DI

AND SAUCES

譜

Cecilia Jennie Au Yang
歐陽紉漸著
Chopsticks Cooking Centre
嘉饌家政中心

博益出版集團有限公司

FOREWORD

In the days when people visited the market daily to buy fresh ingredients, I was already using a freezer to store precooked dishes. A freezer is a blessing for people who enjoy cooking, as raw and cooked meat, vegetables and fruit can be kept for a long time.

A freezer not only saves shopping and cooking time, it also helps save money through bulk buying. I learned this while teaching classes of overseas Chinese how to cook their favourite Chinese soups and sauces.

I often had to prepare large quantities of different sauces and these had to be kept in a freezer. At first, many of my students were surprised because they thought that food kept in a freezer would be tasteless. It was only after discovering that the sauces retained their original flavour that they also wanted to learn this convenient "trick". Years later frozen ready-cooked food could be found in every supermarket. Though beautifully packaged, supermarket convenience food cannot compete with our home-made freezer food when it comes to cost and flavour. The increasing popularity of microwave food made me realise that many people nowadays have decided to trade freshness for convenience. For this reason I have spent nearly two years testing and developing different sauces and their storage methods, marrying flavour with practicality. Frozen sauces are a must for busy working people. Gourmets can enjoy delicious meals even if they are unable to spend much time in the kitchen.

This recipe book is dedicated to readers who love both good food and convenience. Follow my recipes and you will be successful in creating tasty menus.

前言

早在一般人還在天天逛市場，餐餐煮飯菜堅持每頓新鮮的時候，我已經大膽地、反傳統地實行盡量利用電冰箱貯存預早準備之佳餚。對於愛好烹飪的人來說，冰箱實在是一個偉大的發明。它可以把生或熟肉甚至蔬菜水果貯存一個相當長的時期，使主婦們省卻不少買菜及烹煮的時間。如果善用冰箱，不但省時，連金錢也節省不少。

我經常要指導一些歸化了外國而仍熱愛中國美食的學員如何利用冰箱貯存湯水及粥以供其個人享用；另外我更製作大量醬汁方便隨用隨取。此舉當時被許多人視為不可思議。因為他們認為預先煮熟食物貯存是不衛生及沒有營養的，而且沒有味道。可是不知從何時開始，超級市場內之食物架上已經陳列着不少即食飯菜。那些包裝得美輪美奐的盒裝食品，它們的衛生、味道、健康程度又豈能與自己烹煮、預先貯存於冰箱內的食物相比？而價錢更與自製者相距甚遠。就是因為那些即食飯菜啟發了我，使我知道現代人的思想已開放了，大部分人不得不接受現實，放棄每日新鮮之念頭，轉而求取方便之門。於是我用了差不多兩年時間去嘗試及研究各種醬汁的組合、製作及貯存，務求達到美味而方便的目的。其實只要緊守貯存規則，再配上優良的烹調技巧，並在指定時間內用完，急凍冷藏醬汁實在是分秒必爭的職業人士之必需品。尤其是愛好美食之人士，不至因過於忙碌而失卻享用美點佳餚之機會。

謹以此書獻給熱愛美食的人士，希望讀者們皆能利用書內各款醬汁，成功地炮製出更多美點佳餚。

THE AUTHOR 作者簡介

THE AUTHOR

Cecilia Jennie Au-Yang graduated in home economics from Grantham Teacher Training College, Hong Kong, in 1956. Over the years, she studied cooking in her spare time with famous Hong Kong chefs.

In 1971, she founded Chopsticks Cooking Centre to provide the best facilities for teaching Chinese home cooking.

Since 1974, she has taught professional cookery training courses for people interested in working in catering. The courses enable students to learn cooking while working as trainees and gaining work experience. Many graduates from these courses have successfully found employment in the food and catering industries overseas.

Cecilia set up Chopsticks Publications Limited in 1975 to publish her own recipes - the "Chopsticks Recipes" series with one colour photograph per dish and English and Chinese text.

In 1984, Chopsticks Publications Limited entered the UK market when Cecilia co-published a 240-page hardcover Chinese cookery book "The Best of Chinese Cooking" with Hamyln Publishing, England. The following year the book was translated into Dutch.

In 1989, she wrote a series of five popular pocket-sized cookery books for the Japanese publisher, Tokuma Shoten.

To date she has written and published a total of 20 cookery books.

In recent years, Cecilia has also been writing cookery columns for various well-known Hong Kong magazines and newspapers, and has acted as a consultant to several food manufacturers, testing and writing new recipes as well as training sales representatives in using their own products.

Cecilia Au-Yang's cookery books are used worldwide by housewives, gourmets and professional chefs.

歐陽紉澌女士1956年畢業於香港葛量洪教育學院家政系。在其教學生涯中，歐陽女士利用空閒時間努力於研究廚藝。

1971年歐陽女士開始設帳授徒，專門教授家庭小菜。

1974年首創半工讀烹飪培訓班，訓練欲投身飲食業之人士，是項課程對熱愛烹飪人士提供一個良好之學習機會。歷年來之畢業生移居外地經營飲食業而揚威海外者甚眾。

1975年歐陽女士成立嘉饌出版有限公司，首創中英對照、每菜一圖之彩色食譜《美點佳餚》書集。

1984年《美點佳餚》被英國大出版社Hamyln Publishing 購買版權，輯成一本240頁精裝食譜："The Best of Chinese Cooking"。翌年更被翻譯為荷蘭文。

1989年《美點佳餚》進入日本市場，為日本大出版社德間文庫編成五本袋裝食譜。

至今歐陽女士已寫作及出版20本食譜。

近年來，歐陽女士除教授烹飪外，並專心致力為食品公司試驗新產品、設計新食譜及培訓食品推廣人士。

歐陽紉澌女士之食譜深受世界各地的主婦、美食家及職業廚師所歡迎及採用。

CONTENTS

目錄

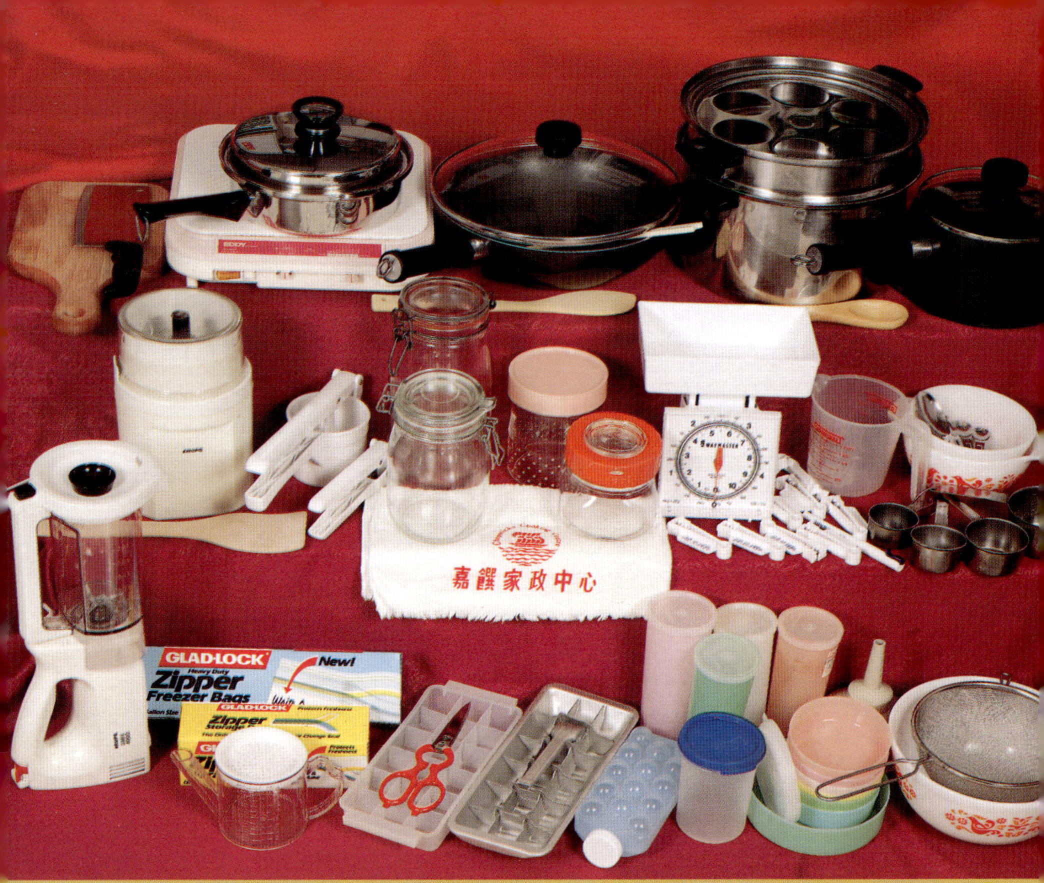

醬汁器皿選用

COOKING UTENSILS FOR DIPS AND SAUCES

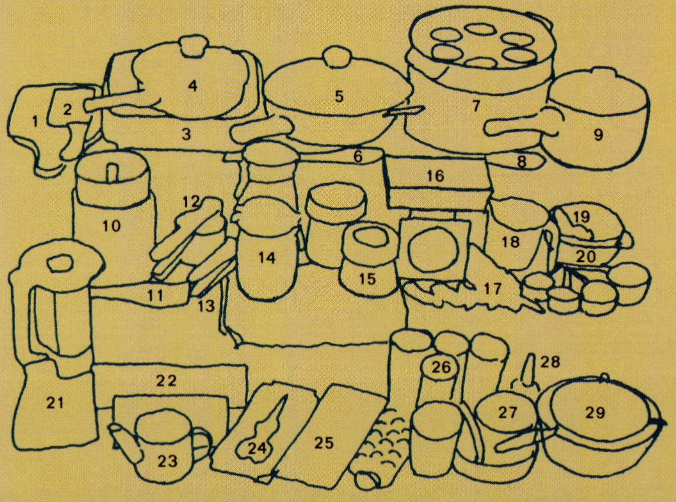

1. Chopping Board 砧板
2. Chopper 刀
3. Induction Cooker 電磁爐
4. Stainless Steel Saucepan 不銹鋼煲
5. Non-stick Pan 易潔煎鑊
6. Wooden Spatula 木鏟
7. Multi-purpose Steamer Set 多用蒸煲
8. Wooden Spoon 木匙
9. Non-stick Saucepan 易潔煲
10. Electric Mini Chopper (Food Processor) 電動碎肉機
11. Wooden Turner 木鑊鏟
12. Fruit Juicer 榨汁器
13. Garlic Press 蒜茸夾
14. Air-tight Jars 密實瓶
15. Glass Jars 玻璃瓶
16. Kitchen Scale 磅
17. Freezer Bag Clips 冰袋夾
18. Measuring Cups 量杯
19. Measuring Spoons 量匙
20. Mixing Bowl 攪拌盆
21. Electric Blender 電動攪拌機
22. Zipper Freezer Bags 密實袋
23. Oil Separator 隔油壺
24. Scissors 剪刀
25. Ice-trays 製冰格
26. Plastic Cups 膠杯
27. Plastic Boxes 膠盒
28. Funnel 漏斗
29. Strainer 疏孔篩

常用中文烹飪用語註釋

編者按：在各款食譜製作方法中，為方便香港各家庭主婦，每每使用粵語常用的烹飪術語，使用其他方言的中國讀者或會感到不明白，編者特於每篇食譜末附加粵語與白話的用詞對照，而於每篇食譜中常出現的粵語用詞，現注解如下：

生抽=淺色醬油
老抽=深色醬油
生粉=太白粉
蒜茸=蒜泥
蔴油=香油
浙醋=紅醋
芫荽=香菜
雪櫃=冰箱
冰箱=冷藏格
鑊=炒鍋
埋獻=勾芡
煲=煮

UTENSILS FOR PREPARING SAUCES

醬汁器皿選用

A sauce is the soul of good food and it can be prepared in a large quantity well in advance. Even if you have little time you can still make a delicious meal. But if the proper utensils are not used, the flavour of a tasty sauce might be affected or ruined. Therefore, all the utensils must be ready before you start preparing sauces.

1. An induction cooker is the best choice as it is clean and simple to use. An electric cooker, a gas cooker or a bottled-gas cooker can also be used, but choose one with automatic ignition for easy control of the heat. Cookers that are difficult to control tend to cause saucepans to boil over, which results in "dried up" sauces.
2. Stainless steel and non-stick saucepans from 1 to 3 litres should be used for preparing different quantities of sauce. Stainless steel cookware can be used with any type of stove. Non-stick pans cannot be used with induction cookers.
3. Steamer sets can be either stainless steel or non-stick. Sauces which cannot be cooked over direct heat should be steamed. A frozen block of sauce can be defrosted in a microwave oven or a steamer.
4. A food processor is easy to clean and is the most time-saving piece of kitchen equipment. It can turn 6 oz (168g) of meat into puree within 10 seconds.
5. A fruit juicer is the best tool for squeezing small quantities of fruit juice, ginger juice or potato puree.
6. A garlic press is easy to use. It saves mincing and chopping the garlic on a chopping board. A blender should be used if a large quantity is needed.
7. Air-tight glass jars are used to store thick and aromatic dips and sauces to prevent their flavour escaping. Glass jars should not be placed in a freezer.
8. Ordinary glass jars or bottles are used for storing sauces at room temperature or in a refrigerator.
9. Clean towels are a must as all containers should be cleaned before use.
10. It is best to choose a kitchen scale with a container on top. The weight must be shown in both ounces and grams.
11. Freezer bag clips are used to seal plastic bags. Mark each bag with the production date of the sauce.
12. There are many varieties of plastic and glass measuring cups in sets of four, from 1/4 cup to 1 cup, and from 1 cup to 4 cup, for example. 1 cup is equivalent to 8 fl oz.

13. A set of four measuring spoons is needed in the most common sizes: 1/4 tsp, 1/2 tsp, 1 tsp and 1 tbsp.

14. Mixing bowls of different sizes are needed for holding and mixing sauces.

15. An electric blender is used for liquidising large quantites of fruit or vegetables.

16. Zipper freezer bags are used for holding frozen sauce cubes.

17. An oil separator is a container used to filter a sauce and pour it into a narrow bottle.

18. Ice-trays can be used to freeze the sauce into cubes, which can be knocked out of the trays and stored in plastic freezer bags.

19. Kitchen scissors can be used for trimming prawns and crabs, and for cutting plastic bags and ice cubes to size.

20. Plastic cups and boxes are used for storing sauces in a freezer.

21. A funnel is used to pour a sauce from the saucepan into a bottle.

醬汁是美食之靈魂，而且可以預早大量烹製以備不時之需，但是如果器皿使用不當，美味的醬汁便會變味甚至腐壞至不能使用，所以在製作之前必須將用具準備妥當。

1. 電磁爐是最簡單乾淨、舒服的首選，其他電爐、石油氣爐、煤氣爐也可以使用，但必須選用自動打火及容易調較高低火力的爐具，否則汁液容易煮乾或滿瀉。

2. 1公升至3公升深淺不銹鋼及易潔鍋可用來烹製不同分量的醬汁。不銹鋼鍋可與任何爐具配合，而易潔鍋不適用於電磁爐。

3. 套裝蒸鍋、不銹鋼或易潔鍋皆可使用，凡不適宜以火直接烹煮的醬汁皆可用蒸籠蒸燉。從冰箱取出雪硬的醬汁，除可用微波爐解凍外，可放蒸籠內燉至完全軟化，將醬汁還原。

4. 碎肉機是最迅速之廚房助手，可把6安士肉類在10秒鐘內攪成肉茸，快速而乾淨。

5. 榨汁器適宜用來榨取小量果汁、薑汁或薯泥等。

6. 蒜茸夾可省卻用刀在砧板上剁蒜茸的麻煩，但只宜小量製作，大量製作可用攪拌器。

7. 密實玻璃瓶適宜用以盛載濃味醬汁，使氣味不容易流失，但不宜放入冰箱。

8. 普通玻璃瓶用於貯存在雪櫃或室溫中的濃醬。

9. 毛巾是做醬汁前必須準備的用品，因一切器皿皆需拭抹後才使用。

10. 磅須選用有盛器在上，而且包括有安士（英制）及克（公制）重量指示的。

11. 封膠袋夾子用於將膠袋封口及註明製作日期。

12. 量杯有1至4杯裝及1/4至1杯四隻套裝，1量杯相等流質8安士。

13. 量匙通常四隻一套：1/4茶匙、1/2茶匙、1茶匙及1湯匙。

14. 深盆不同大小數個用以調拌醬料。

15. 密實袋用以盛載冰成硬粒之醬汁。

16. 隔油壺，把汁液轉盛在窄口瓶時，使用隔油壺令汁液容易注入，同時隔去渣滓。

17. 製冰格可把汁冰硬後分成小粒，放於密實袋中，容易取用。

18. 剪刀除用以剪蝦、蟹爪外，可用作剪開膠袋甚至冰塊。

19. 膠杯及膠盒用以盛載貯存於冰箱內之醬汁。

20. 漏斗用以將汁液轉盛於窄口瓶中。

21. 篩可選用略疏孔的，用以將渣滓隔出。

Cha Shiu Paste 叉燒醬

叉燒醬

Ingredients:
3 slices ginger
1 oz (28g) shallot or onion
1 oz (28g) garlic
2 cups ground bean paste
2 cups hoi sin paste
1 cup sesame paste or peanut butter
3 tbsp sesame oil
2 tbsp rose wine or sherry
1/2 cup Stock (P.101)
Seasoning:
1 tsp spicy salt
1 cup light soy
1 1/2 cups sugar
1/4 cup red colouring solution
Finished Product:
7 cups
Storage Time:
1 month at room temperature
6 months in a refrigerator
Method:
* Scrape, wash and slice the ginger. Peel, wash and slice the shallot and garlic. Place these ingredients in a food processor and mince finely, then pour them into a bowl.
* Mix the 3 kinds of paste in a small bowl and stir well. Set aside for later use.
* Heat the wok and bring the sesame oil to the boil. Saute the minced ingredients until aromatic. Stir in the mixed pastes and fry for a few seconds. Sizzle the wine, add the Stock and seasoning and turn off the heat. Leave to cool and keep in a jar.
Usage:
* This sauce can be blended with Stock and light soy and used as a cha shiu or roast pork marinade, or mixed with the juice from roast pork and poured on steamed rice or noodles. It is also used for stewing chicken and duck, or stir frying shredded pork.

材料：
薑3片
葱頭1安士（28克）
蒜頭1安士（28克）
磨豉醬2杯
海鮮醬2杯
蔴醬或花生醬1杯
蔴油3湯匙
玫瑰露酒2湯匙
上湯1/2杯（第101頁）
調味：
香鹽1茶匙
生抽1杯
糖1 1/2杯
紅粉水1/4杯
製成品：
7杯
貯存期：
室溫1月
雪櫃6月
製法：
* 薑切絲，葱頭、蒜頭去衣洗淨切片，將全部材料放入攪拌機內攪成茸後，取出置小碗內。
* 將三種醬料一同放在另一碗內拌勻候用。
* 燒紅鑊，加入蔴油煮沸，爆香薑、葱頭及蒜頭，拌入混合醬料炒數秒鐘，灒酒，加上湯及調味料，試妥味後，取出待凍，盛在瓶內候用。
用途：
* 此醬除可加生抽、上湯用以醃製叉燒外，亦可爆炒雞鴨等。若與燒叉燒之肉汁和勻，即可當淋飯、麪之汁液用。

Cha Shiu (Barbecued Pork)

蜜汁叉燒

蜜汁叉燒

Ingredients:

1 lb (1/2 kg) pork loin
2 slices ginger
2 shallots
2 cloves garlic
1/2 cup Cha Shiu Paste (P.13)
1/2 cup light soy
1/4 cup Stock (P.101)
1/4 cup sugar

Coating:

1/4 cup water
1 cup syrup

Method:

* Cut the pork loin into 4 long strips and pat with the blade of a meat cleaver.

* Mince the ginger, shallots and garlic and mix with all the other ingredients. Marinate the pork strips for 50 minutes, turning them over every 10 minutes.

* Remove the pork strips from the marinade and put them on a greased rack in a baking tin. Place in a preheated oven 230°C (450 °F, gas mark 8) and roast for 15 minutes.

* Meanwhile, bring the 1/4 cup water to the boil in a saucepan. Stir in the syrup and simmer until it thickens.

* Remove the pork strips from the oven. Dip each piece thoroughly in the cooked syrup. Return the pork to the oven and continue to roast for another 10 minutes.

* Take the pork out again and coat with syrup for a second time. Increase the heat to 260° C (500 °F, gas mark 9), turn the pork over and roast the other side for a final 5 minutes. Remove and slice the pork strips. Serve hot or cold.

材料：

枚肉1磅（1/2公斤）
薑2片
葱頭2粒
蒜頭2粒
叉燒醬1/2杯（第13頁）
生抽1/2杯
上湯1/4杯（第101頁）
糖1/4杯

淋料：

水1/4杯
糖膠1杯

製法：

* 枚肉洗淨，分切4條，以刀略拍鬆。

* 薑、葱頭及蒜頭剁茸，與叉燒醬、生抽、上湯及糖一同拌勻，調至合味，把肉條放入醃50分鐘，每10分鐘反身1次。

* 將肉取出，放在已塗油的烤架上，置已預熱230℃（450℉，煤氣8度）之焗爐內燒約15分鐘後取出。

* 水與糖膠煮溶，淋在叉燒上，將叉燒反轉再入爐燒約10分鐘，淋第二次糖膠後反轉，加猛火至260℃（500℉，煤氣9度），再燒約5分鐘即成。切片上碟。

Cheese and Cream Sauce
芝士奶油汁

芝士奶油汁

Ingredients:
4 oz (112g) butter
2 tsp minced garlic
2 cups fresh cream
2 oz (56g) Parmesan cheese
4 oz (112g) grated cheddar cheese
1/2 tsp salt
1/2 tsp pepper
Finished Product:
2 cups
Storage Time:
3 days in a refrigerator
1 month in a freezer
Method:
* Dissolve the butter in a frying pan over low heat. Spoon out just the clear melted butter and pour it into a small bowl. Clean the frying pan and return the clear melted butter to it. Saute the garlic until aromatic. Pour in the fresh cream, stir evenly and turn off the heat.
* Blend in the rest of the ingredients and mix thoroughly to a smooth cream. Filter into a clean bowl through a fine sieve and leave to cool. Store in a jar.
Usage:
* Cheese and Cream Sauce can be served with Western dishes and goes particularly well with pasta. It can also be poured on to a casserole before baking. The melted sauce turns an appetising golden brown colour.

材料：
牛油4安士（112克）
蒜茸2茶匙
奶油2杯
芝士粉2安士（56克）
卡夫芝士茸4安士（112克）
鹽1/2茶匙
胡椒粉1/2茶匙
製成品：
2杯
貯存期：
雪櫃3天
冰箱1月
製法：
* 牛油放鍋中以文火煮溶，濾出清牛油用以爆香蒜茸，加入奶油，拌勻後離火。
* 芝士粉及其餘材料傾入鍋中，邊加邊攪至完全和勻及軟滑，試妥味，以疏孔篩隔去雜質，晾凍入瓶候用。
用途：
* 芝士汁除用以調配西式麪食外，可淋於菜餚面上入爐焗至金黃色。
註：卡夫芝士=車打起士

Cauliflower in Cheese Sauce
芝士扒菜花

芝士扒菜花

Ingredients:
1 lb (1/2kg) cauliflower
3 cups salted water
2 tbsp oil
2 tsp minced garlic
1/4 cup Stock (P.101)
1 tbsp butter
3/4 cup Cheese and Cream Sauce (P.17)
1 tbsp minced Chinese ham
1 tbsp minced parsley

Seasoning:
1 tsp wine
1/4 tsp salt
1/4 tsp pepper

Method:
* Cut the cauliflower into small florets. Bring the salted water to the boil in a saucepan over medium heat. Drop in the cauliflower and simmer for 5 minutes. Refresh and drain.
* Heat a wok over medium heat and bring the oil to the boil. Saute the garlic and cooked cauliflower for 2 minutes. Add the Stock and stir fry for about 10 seconds. Pour into a casserole.
* Melt the butter in a saucepan over low heat. Blend the Cheese and Cream Sauce with the seasoning in a separate bowl and stream the mixture into the saucepan. Mix thoroughly, bring to the boil and pour over the cauliflower. Sprinkle the minced Chinese ham and parsley on top and serve in the casserole dish.

材料：
椰菜花1磅（1/2公斤）
沸鹽水3杯
油2湯匙
蒜茸2茶匙
上湯1/4杯（第101頁）
牛油1湯匙
芝士奶油汁3/4杯（第17頁）
金華火腿茸1湯匙
芫荽茸1湯匙

調味：
酒1茶匙
鹽1/4茶匙
胡椒粉1/4茶匙

製法：
* 椰菜花切小棵，以鹽水浸片刻，轉放沸鹽水中煮5分鐘，沖凍，隔去水分。
* 鑊燒熱，加油煮沸，爆香蒜茸及椰菜花，即將上湯邊灑邊炒十數秒，轉盛瓦砵內。
* 牛油放在小鍋內煮溶，調味料與芝士奶油汁混和傾入煮沸，調妥味，淋在椰菜花上，再灑上火腿茸及芫荽茸即成。

註：椰菜花=白花菜　芝士=起士

Chilli Soy Sauce
辣椒豉油

Ingredients:
3 slices ginger
4 shallots
4 red chillies
1/4 cup oil
1 tbsp wine
2 cups dark soy
1/2 cup sugar
2 tbsp sesame oil
2 sprigs parsley
Finished Product:
2 cups
Storage Time:
1 month at room temperature
3 months in a refrigerator
Method:
* Mash the ginger and shallots. Wash and shred the red chillies.Wash, trim and cut the parsley finely.
* Heat a saucepan and bring the oil to the boil. Saute the ginger and shallots and discard. Sizzle the wine and stir in the soy and sugar. Adjust the flavour to taste, return to the boil and turn off the heat. Sprinkle in the chillies and sesame oil. Leave to cool and store in a jar.
Usage:
* This sauce is best served as a dip for seafood such as steamed prawns or fish balls. It also goes well with rice or noodles. Add chopped parsley to the sauce before serving.

辣椒豉油

材料：
薑3片
葱頭4粒
紅椒4隻
油1/4杯
酒1湯匙
老抽2杯
糖1/2杯
麻油2湯匙
芫荽2棵（用時加入）
製成品：
2杯
貯存期：
室溫1月
雪櫃3月
製法：
* 薑片、葱頭拍扁，紅椒洗淨切絲，芫荽洗淨修妥切細。
* 不銹鋼煲燒紅，放入油煮沸，隨即放入薑、葱頭爆香，棄去。灒酒，傾入老抽及糖，試至合味，再煮沸後離火，灑下紅椒絲及麻油，晾凍，倒入窄口瓶內，隨時取食。
用途：
* 此汁最適宜與海鮮配合，如白灼蝦、鯪魚球等。亦可與飯、麪等配合及作點食醬油。用時方加芫荽。

Steamed Fresh Shrimp

籠仔蒸生蝦

籠仔蒸生蝦

Ingredients:

1 lb (1/2kg) fresh shrimps
2 tbsp oil
2 tbsp shredded ginger
1 tsp wine
1/2 cup Chilli Soy Sauce (P.21)
1 tbsp shredded red chilli
2 tbsp shredded spring onion

Method:

* Wash the shrimps and place into a steamer sitting on 1/2 wok of water. Bring the water to the boil over high heat for 3 minutes. Remove and serve in the steamer.

* Heat a wok and bring the oil to the boil. Saute the ginger until pungent then sizzle in the wine and pour in the Chilli Soy Sauce. When it reboils, add the chilli and spring onion. Dish and serve as a dip with the shrimps.

材料：

生蝦1磅（1/2公斤）
油2湯匙
薑絲2湯匙
酒1茶匙
辣椒豉油1/2杯（第21頁）
紅椒絲1湯匙
葱絲2湯匙

製法：

* 生蝦洗淨後放蒸籠內，置半鑊沸水之上以大火蒸3分鐘，取出原籠上桌。

* 燒紅鑊，將油傾入，爆香薑絲，濳酒，加入辣椒豉油煮沸，即下紅椒絲及葱絲和勻，以小碟盛載與蝦同上。

Chinese Salad Dressing
涼拌汁

涼拌汁

Ingredients:
1 oz (28g) garlic
1 oz (28g) Chinese celery
2/3 cup Stock (P.101)
1/2 cup light soy
2/3 cup red vinegar
1/4 cup sugar
4 tbsp hot broad bean paste
2 tbsp sesame oil

Finished Product:
2 cups

Storage Time:
1 month in a refrigerator
3 months in a freezer

Method:
* Peel the garlic, wash and mince it with the celery.
* Pour the Stock, light soy, red vinegar and sugar into a mixing bowl. Blend in the garlic, celery and hot broad bean paste and adjust the seasoning. Sprinkle in the sesame oil and mix well.
* Store the Chinese Salad Dressing in a glass bottle marked with the date of production and keep in a refrigerator or freezer.

Usage:
* Chinese Salad Dressing is best mixed with plain cooked food such as poached ox-tongue, boiled bean curd or steamed vegetables. To enhance its flavour, this dressing can be mixed with other rich, crispy and fragrant ingredients such as minced Chinese ham, coarsely chopped deep fried walnuts, minced parsley and diced spring onion.

材料：
蒜頭1安士（28克）
中芹1安士（28克）
上湯2/3杯（第101頁）
生抽1/2杯
浙醋2/3杯
糖1/4杯
豆瓣醬4湯匙
蔴油2湯匙

製成品：
2杯

貯存期：
雪櫃1月
冰箱3月

製法：
* 蒜頭去衣，與中芹洗淨，剁爛成茸。
* 將上湯、生抽、浙醋、糖放入大盆內拌勻，加入蒜芹茸及豆瓣醬，攪拌後試至合味，最後流入蔴油拌勻即成。
* 將製成品注入玻璃瓶中，註明製造日期，放於雪櫃或冰箱內候用。

用途：
* 此汁適用於淥熟的材料如牛脷、豆腐或生切蔬菜等，能引起食欲。取用時可酌加辛香材料如芫荽、葱茸，或香濃材料如火腿茸，酥脆材料如炸合桃碎等拌勻配食。

註：牛脷＝牛舌

Summer Rainbow Salad
夏日彩虹

夏日彩虹

Ingredients:
1 light green capsicum
1 dark green capsicum
1 red capsicum
1 yellow capsicum
1 purple capsicum
2 oz (56g) carrot
2 packets konjac threads
4 oz (112g) ham
1 oz (28g) candied walnuts
1 tbsp red chilli rings to garnish
3/4 cup Chinese Salad Dressing (P.25)

Method:
* Deseed and shred all the capsicums. Peel, shred, blanch and refresh the carrot.
* Blanch the konjac threads in 3 cups of salted water for 1 minute, refresh and drain. Shred the ham and coarsely chop the candied walnuts.
* Arrange the ham and vegetables on a flat plate, with the konjac threads in the centre and sprinkle the red chilli rings all over the dish.
* Pour the cold Chinese Salad Dressing evenly on the konjac threads and vegetables. Scatter the chopped walnuts on top.

材料：
深、淺綠椒各1隻
紅椒1隻
黃椒1隻
紫椒1隻
紅蘿蔔2安士（56克）
魔芋絲2包
火腿4 安士（112克）
琥珀合桃1安士（28克）
紅椒圈1湯匙（裝飾）
涼拌汁3/4杯（第25頁）

製法：
* 各色椒去籽切絲。紅蘿蔔去皮切絲，放入沸水中略浸後，過凍。
* 魔芋絲放於3杯鹽水中煮1分鐘後沖洗乾淨。火腿切絲，合桃剁碎。
* 將各色蔬菜及火腿絲排妥於平碟上。魔芋絲堆放中央，紅椒圈點綴。
* 涼拌汁和勻，淋在蔬菜及魔芋絲上，灑下合桃碎即可上桌。

Chiu Chow Chilli Oil
潮州辣油

潮州辣油

Ingredients:
4 oz (112g) dried chillies
4 oz (112g) garlic
3 cups oil

Finished Product:
3 cups

Storage Time:
1 month at room temperature
3 months in a refrigerator

Method:
* Wash and wipe the dried chillies. Peel and slice the garlic.
* Heat a wok and bring 2 cups oil to the boil. Drop in the garlic and chillies and deep fry over medium heat until pungent and crisp.
* Remove the chillies and garlic from the oil and drain. Pound the ingredients in a mortar until fine. Place the powder in a jar, pour in the remaining cup of oil and stir until thoroughly mixed.
* The oil used for deep frying the chillies can either be poured into the same jar, or stored separately for use as a dip or for cooking.

Usage:
* The Chiu Chow Chilli Oil can be poured over Noodles or Rice Sticks with Fish Balls (P.31), or cooked with soya sauce and sugar to make a dip for seafood.

材料：
辣椒乾4安士（112克）
蒜肉4安士（112克）
油3杯

製成品：
3杯

貯存期：
室溫1月
雪櫃3月

製法：
* 用濕布將辣椒抹淨，蒜肉切片。
* 燒紅鑊，將2杯油慢火煮沸，放入蒜片及辣椒，以中火炸至香脆。
* 以漏勺把蒜片、辣椒盛出，搗成茸，放入大口瓶，將餘油1杯傾入拌勻。
* 炸過蒜片、辣椒之熱油可以晾凍，傾回辣椒茸瓶內和勻，亦可另以小瓶盛起，用以煮菜或作蘸汁用。

用途：
* 此辣油除與魚蛋粉同食外，亦可作海鮮蘸料。加豉油及糖同煮，即成為另一款點食汁。

Rice Sticks with Fish Balls in Soup 魚蛋粉

魚蛋粉

Ingredients:
6 oz (168g) fish balls
8 oz (224g) rice sticks
2 tbsp garlic vegetable
2 tbsp oil
2 slices ginger
2 tbsp Chiu Chow Chilli Oil (P.29) (served as a dip)

Seasoning:
1 tsp wine
3 cups Fish Stock (P.47)
1/4 tsp salt
1/4 tsp pepper
1 tsp sesame oil

Method:
* Wash the fish balls, rice sticks and garlic vegetable separately.
* Heat a wok over medium heat and bring the oil to the boil, saute the ginger until pungent, then discard. Sizzle the wine, stream in the Fish Stock and bring to the boil again. Blanch the rice sticks then instantly ladle them into serving bowls. Sprinkle the garlic vegetable on top.
* Place the fish balls in the wok and boil them in the same Stock for 30 seconds. Drain the Stock into a small bowl and arrange the fish balls on the rice sticks.
* Stir the remaining seasoning into the Stock, mix well and adjust the flavour to taste. Pour onto the rice sticks. Serve the Chiu Chow Chilli Oil as a dip.

材料：
魚蛋6安士（168克）
河粉8安士（224克）
冬菜2湯匙
油2湯匙
薑2片
辣椒油2湯匙（配食）（第29頁）

調味：
酒1茶匙
魚上湯3杯（第47頁）
鹽1/4茶匙
胡椒粉1/4茶匙
蔴油1茶匙

製法：
* 魚蛋、河粉及冬菜分別洗淨候用。
* 鑊燒熱，加油煮沸，爆香薑片棄去，灒酒，加上湯煮沸，即可將河粉傾下浸泡，立即盛起，分置兩碗中，冬菜分為二份灑在河粉上。
* 魚蛋傾入上湯內煮1/2分鐘，盛起分放兩碗河粉上。
* 其餘調味加上湯內試至合味，即可傾在粉碗中上桌，以辣椒油伴食。

Curry Sauce
咖喱汁

咖喱汁

Ingredients:
2 oz (56g) curry powder
8 tbsp oil
4 red chillies
10 oz (280g) shallot
4 oz (112g) onion
1 sprig lemon grass
1 cup coconut milk

Seasoning:
2 tsp wine
2 cups Stock (P.101)
1/4 tsp salt
1/4 cup light soy
2 tbsp sugar
2 tsp chicken powder

Finished Product:
5 cups

Storage Time:
1 week in a refrigerator
3 months in a freezer

Method:
* Place the curry powder and 4 tbsp of the oil in a bowl. Mix well into a paste and set aside for later use.
* Deseed and dice the chillies. Peel and dice the shallot and onion. Dice the lemon grass. Put all these ingredients into a food processor, add half the Stock and blend into a puree.
* Heat the wok and bring the remaining oil to the boil. Saute the chillies and shallot puree over low heat until fragrant. Add the curry paste and saute until aromatic. Sizzle the wine, pour in the coconut milk, the remaining cup of Stock and the rest of the seasoning. Adjust the flavour to taste, turn off the heat and leave to cool.

Usage:
* This sauce can be used with many meat and poultry dishes, including Blanched Beef and Chinese Roast Chicken. It can also be mixed with noodles or used in braised chicken wing and spare rib casserole dishes.

材料：
咖喱粉2安士（56克）
油8湯匙
紅椒4隻
葱頭10安士（280克）
洋葱4安士（112克）
香茅1枝
椰汁1杯

調味：
酒2茶匙
上湯2杯（第101頁）
鹽1/4茶匙
生抽1/4杯
糖2湯匙
雞粉2茶匙

製成品：
5杯

貯存期：
雪櫃1周
冰箱3月

製法：
* 將咖喱粉放入碗中，加油4湯匙和勻候用。
* 紅椒去籽，葱頭、洋葱去衣一同切小件，香茅切碎，一同放入攪拌機內，加一半上湯攪成醬。
* 鑊燒紅，加入餘油煮沸，將紅椒、葱頭醬傾入，以慢火炒香，加咖喱醬續炒至香味四溢時，灒酒，再加餘下上湯、調味料及椰汁，試妥味後隨即停火，晾凍待用。

用途：
* 此汁可淋於各式熟肉如白灼牛肉、燒雞等之上，亦可用以燜製雞翼、排骨及拌麪等，用途甚廣。

Curry Salmon Head
咖喱三文魚頭

咖喱三文魚頭

Ingredients:
1 salmon head
1/2 cup cornflour
1/2 wok oil
3 slices ginger
2 shallots
2 cloves garlic
1 spring onion
8 new potatoes
Marinade:
1 tbsp ginger juice
2 tbsp light soy
1 tsp sugar
1/2 tsp pepper
Seasoning:
1 tbsp wine
1 1/2 cup Curry Sauce (P.33)
Method:
* Wash and cut the salmon head into bite-sized pieces. Mix well with the marinade, set aside for 20 minutes then coat evenly with cornflour. Bring the oil to the boil, slide in the fish head and deep fry until golden brown. Drain the oil into a container.
* Mash the ginger, shallots and garlic. Section the spring onion. Boil the new potatoes for 10 minutes, then peel and cut into halves.
* Heat a wok and bring 2 tbsp of the drained oil to the boil again. Saute the mashed ginger, shallots and garlic until aromatic. Sizzle the wine and stir in the Curry Sauce. Add the fish head and bring to the boil. Cover and simmer for 10 minutes. Stir in the potatoes, cook for another 5 minutes, then season to taste. Scatter the sectioned spring onion on top, dish and serve immediately.

材料：
三文魚頭1個
生粉1/2杯
油1/2鑊
薑3片
葱頭2粒
蒜頭2粒
葱1條
新馬鈴薯8個
醃料：
薑汁1湯匙
生抽2湯匙
糖1茶匙
胡椒粉1/2茶匙
調味：
酒1湯匙
咖喱汁1 1/2杯（第33頁）
製法：
* 三文魚頭洗淨抹乾斬件，用和勻醃料醃20分鐘後，撲上生粉。將油煮沸，放入魚頭以中火炸至金黃色，盛起隔去餘油。
* 薑、葱頭及蒜頭拍扁，葱切段。馬鈴薯用沸水煮熟，每個去皮切開兩邊。
* 鑊中餘油2湯匙煮沸，爆香薑、葱頭及蒜頭，灒酒，將咖喱汁傾下，加入魚頭煮沸，蓋密續煮10分鐘，加入馬鈴薯拌勻，煮5分鐘，試妥味，加入葱段即可上碟。

Fermented Red Bean Curd Paste
蒜茸南乳醬

蒜茸南乳醬

Ingredients:
1/4 oz (7g) ginger
1 oz (28g) garlic
2 tbsp sesame oil
3/4 cup fermented red bean curd
1 tbsp wine
1/2 cup Stock (P.101)
3/4 cup sugar
2 chicken cubes
1/2 cup mashed parsley

Finished Product:
3 cups

Storage Time:
1 month in a refrigerator
3 months in a freezer

Method:
* Peel and slice the ginger and garlic. Mince together in a food processor.
* Heat the wok and bring the sesame oil to the boil. Saute the ginger and garlic puree until aromatic. Stir in the fermented red bean curd and simmer over low heat for 10 seconds. Sizzle the wine. Pour in the Stock and reboil. Add the sugar and chicken cubes, adjust the seasoning, then remove and set aside to cool. Store in a jar.
* Mix with the mashed parsley before serving.

Usage:
* Fermented Red Bean Curd Paste can be used as a marinade for roasts such as chicken and spare ribs, or added to Stock and served as a dip.

材料：
薑1/4安士（7克）
蒜頭1安士（28克）
蔴油2湯匙
南乳3/4杯
酒1湯匙
上湯1/2杯（第101頁）
糖3/4杯
鷄精2粒
芫荽茸1/2杯

製成品：
3杯

貯存期：
雪櫃1月
冰箱3月

製法：
* 薑、蒜頭去衣切片，一同放在攪肉機內攪爛成茸。
* 燒紅鑊，加入蔴油煮沸，傾入薑、蒜茸爆香，即將南乳搗爛加入，以慢火同煮約10秒鐘，灒酒，將上湯流入煮至重沸時，再加入糖及鷄精，試妥味即離火，晾凍入瓶。使用時加入芫荽茸拌勻。

用途：
* 南乳醬除用於醃製燒鷄、燒排骨外，可酌加上湯開稀作蘸食之醬汁。

註：南乳＝紅腐乳

Roast Chicken with Fermented Red Bean Curd Paste 南乳吊燒鷄

南乳吊燒雞

Ingredients:
1 chicken about 3 lb (1 1/2 kg)
1 cup Fermented Red Bean Curd Paste (P.37)
1 oz (28g) dried lily buds
1/4 cup water
1 tsp sugar
1/2 wok oil
2 sprigs trimmed parsley

Coating Ingredients:
1 1/4 cups white vinegar
3 oz (84g) maltose
1/4 cup red vinegar

Method:
* Wash and dry the chicken. Brush 1/2 cup of the Fermented Red Bean Curd Paste inside the chicken and marinate for 30 minutes.
* Soak and drain the dried lily buds, then mix well with the water, sugar, and 1/4 cup of the Fermented Red Bean Curd Paste. Stuff the chicken with the mixture and sew up the opening with a skewer.
* Bring 1/2 wok water to the boil and steam the chicken over the water for 20 minutes. Pour the hot water over the cooked chicken to remove the fat on the skin.
* Mix the coating ingredients in a wok and simmer until dissolved, then pour the sauce over the cooked chicken. Hang it up to dry for about 8 hours.
* Heat the oil and bring to the boil. Deep fry the chicken until golden brown. Drain the excess oil.
* Heat the remaining 1/4 cup of Fermented Red Bean Curd Paste with 2 tbsp water and bring to the boil. Serve as a dip.
* Chop the chicken in half, remove the lily buds and place them on a platter. Cut the chicken into bite-sized pieces and arrange them on the lily buds. Sprinkle the parsley over the chicken and serve with the dip.

材料：
光雞1隻約3磅（1 1/2公斤）
蒜茸南乳醬1杯（第37頁）
金針1安士（28克）
水1/4杯
糖1茶匙
油1/2鍋
芫荽2棵（摘妥）

塗皮料：
白醋1 1/4杯
麥芽糖3安士（84克）
浙醋1/4杯

製法：
* 光雞洗淨抹乾，以1/2杯蒜茸南乳醬擦匀雞內腔，醃約1/2小時。
* 金針放水中浸透後隔乾，加水、糖及1/4杯南乳醬一同拌匀，釀入雞腔內，再用鐵針封口。
* 半鑊水煮沸，將雞隔水蒸20分鐘，蒸熟後用鑊中沸水淋在雞上，以沖去表皮油分。
* 塗皮料置鑊中慢火煮溶後，淋於雞身上，吊起吹約8小時至乾。
* 油煮沸後，放入雞炸至金黃色，盛起隔淨餘油。
* 1/4杯蒜茸南乳醬放鑊中，加水2湯匙煮沸，作為蘸汁伴食。
* 把雞斬開兩邊，取出金針，置碟中央，再將雞斬件，排妥於碟上，以芫荽伴碟即成，雞與蘸汁同上桌。

註：南乳=紅腐乳　麥芽糖=飴糖

南乳吊燒雞製作過程

STEP BY STEP - ROAST CHICKEN WITH FERMENTED RED BEAN CURD PASTE

1

2

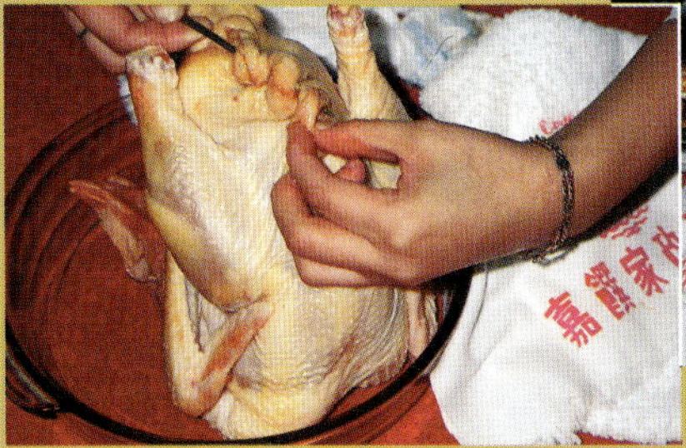

3

4

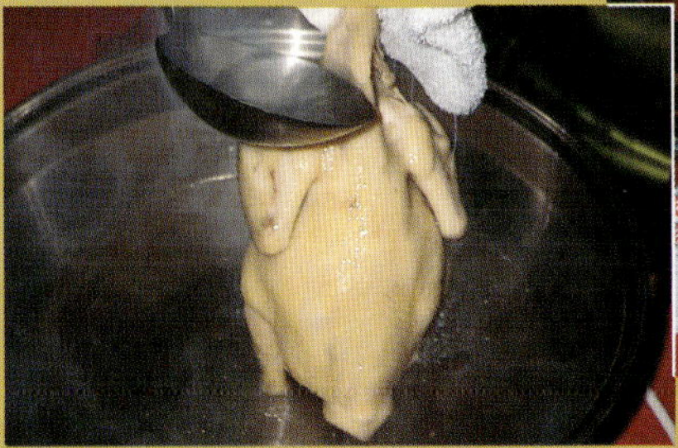

5

6

7

8

9

10

11

12

1. Soak the lily buds until soft and then mix with the Fermented Red Bean Curd Paste.
2. Stuff the chicken with the seasoned lily buds.
3. Steam the stuffed chicken over boiling water for 20 minutes.
4. Pour boiling water over the cooked chicken.
5. After the skin has dried, deep fry the chicken until golden brown.
6. Remove the stuffing from the chicken and place on a platter.
7. Chop the chicken back into pieces, then arrange them in the centre of the platter.
8. Chop the chicken thighs into bite-sized pieces and arrange them on either side of the platter.
9. Remove the bones from the chicken breast and cut the meat into pieces. Arrange them on the left and right side of the platter.
10. Chop up the chicken wings and arrange them between the chicken thighs and breasts.
11. Press the chicken fillets, then place them on either side of the chicken back.
12. The finished dish is Roast Chicken with Fermented Red Bean Curd Paste.

1. 浸軟金針，加入蒜茸南乳醬拌勻。
2. 將和勻金針釀入雞腔內。
3. 釀妥之雞置沸水上蒸20分鐘。
4. 雞蒸熟後以沸水淋於雞身上。
5. 塗皮吊乾後，將雞炸至金黃色。
6. 雞腔內金針取出，排於碟中央。
7. 先把雞背斬件，排在碟中央。
8. 繼將雞腿斬件，排於碟兩旁。
9. 雞胸去骨後斬件，排在碟上左右兩邊。
10. 雞翼斬後，排放於雞腿及雞胸之間。
11. 雞柳拍薄，排於雞背兩側。
12. 「南乳吊燒雞」完成圖

Fermented Red Bean Curd Sauce

南乳香汁

南乳香汁

Ingredients:
2 tbsp sesame oil
1/2 tsp minced ginger
1 tbsp minced garlic
1/4 cup yellow wine
1 1/4 cups Stock (P.101)
4 tbsp fermented red bean curd
1/2 cup chilli tomato sauce
1 tbsp sugar
1 tbsp minced parsley

Finished Product:
2 cups

Storage Time:
1 month in a refrigerator
3 months in a freezer

Method:
* Heat a wok and bring the sesame oil to the boil. Turn off the heat and pour in the minced ginger and garlic. Fry until aromatic. Sizzle in the wine and pour in the Stock.
* Put in the fermented red bean curd, chilli tomato sauce and sugar and bring to the boil. Adjust the flavour to taste. Leave to cool and store in an airtight jar for future use. Add the minced parsley before serving.

Usage:
* This sauce is best when served with plain boiled meat of any type. It can also be used as a dip.

材料：
蔴油2湯匙
薑茸1/2茶匙
蒜茸1湯匙
紹酒1/4杯
上湯1 1/4杯（第101頁）
南乳4湯匙
辣椒茄醬1/2杯
糖1湯匙
芫荽茸1湯匙

製成品：
2杯

貯存期：
雪櫃1月
冰箱3月

製法：
* 鍋燒熱，傾下蔴油煮沸，停火，將薑茸及蒜茸倒入拌勻，灒酒後，即下上湯續拌。
* 南乳、茄醬及糖加入上湯中，以文火煮沸，試至合味，晾凍入瓶。食時方加入芫荽茸。

用途：
* 此汁最宜淋於任何白灼肉之上，亦可作醃料蘸汁用。

Vermicelli with Sliced Pork in Soup 炸肉片米粉

炸肉片米粉

Ingredients:
8 oz (224g) pork loin
8 oz (224g) vermicelli
1/2 tsp minced ginger
1 tsp minced shallot
1 tsp minced garlic
4 cups oil
4 oz (112g) green vegetables
1/4 cup chopped deep fried walnuts
2 tbsp minced parsley

Marinade:
2 tbsp Stock (P.101)
1/4 cup Fermented Red Bean Curd Sauce (P.43)
1 tsp light soy
2 tsp cornflour
1 tsp sesame oil

Seasoning:
1 tsp wine
4 cups Stock (P.101)
1/2 tsp salt
1 tsp chicken powder
1/2 tsp pepper

Method:
* Cut the pork into 1/4 inch (6mm) thick pieces. Soak the vermicelli in hot water, then wash and drain.
* Place the ginger, shallot and garlic into a small bowl and mix with the marinade. Adjust the flavour to taste. Place the pork in the marinade for 20 minutes. Turn and marinate it for a further 20 minutes.
* Heat a wok and bring the oil to the boil. Slide in the pork slices and deep fry them until hardened. Drain and set aside for later use.
* Reboil 2 tbsp of the same oil in the wok, pour in the wine and let it sizzle. Immediately add the Stock and bring it to the boil. Pour in the vermicelli, boil for 2 minutes and loosen it with a pair of chopsticks.Drop in the green vegetables and the rest of the seasoning and mix well. Adjust the flavour to taste and reboil. Ladle into individual bowls. Place the pork slices on the vermicelli and sprinkle the walnuts and parsley on top. Serve hot.

材料：
肉眼8安士（224克）
米粉8安士（224克）
薑茸1/2茶匙
葱頭茸1茶匙
蒜頭茸1茶匙
油4杯
油菜4安士（112克）
炸合桃碎1/4杯
芫荽茸2湯匙

醃肉料：
上湯2湯匙（第101頁）
南乳香汁1/4杯（第43頁）
生抽1茶匙
生粉2茶匙
蔴油1茶匙

調味：
酒1茶匙
上湯4杯（第101頁）
鹽1/2茶匙
鷄粉1茶匙
胡椒粉1/2茶匙

製法：
* 肉眼切1/4吋（0.6公分）厚片，米粉用熱水浸透洗淨。
* 薑、葱頭、蒜茸放小碗中，加入醃料拌匀，試至合味，把肉片傾下拌匀醃20分鐘，反轉再醃20分鐘。
* 鑊燒熱，將油倒下煮至僅沸時，把肉片滑入鑊中泡炸至硬身，即可盛起隔油候用。
* 原鑊餘油2湯匙再燒沸，濳酒，加上湯煮沸，將隔乾水分之米粉傾下煮2分鐘，以筷子挑散，隨即把菜及調味加入拌匀，試妥味，煮至重沸時即可盛在碗中，肉片排放在粉上，灑下合桃及芫荽茸上桌。

註：肉眼=里脊肉

Fish Stock
魚上湯

魚上湯

Ingredients:
2 lb (1kg) fish bones
6 oz (168g) water chestnuts
6 oz (168g) sugar cane
6 oz (168g) celery
3 tbsp oil
4 slices ginger
2 tbsp yellow wine
3 tbsp peppercorn
16 cups water

Seasoning:
2 tsp salt
2 chicken cubes

Finished Product:
10 cups

Storage Time:
3 days in a refrigerator
2 months in a freezer

Method:
* Wash and dry the fish bones. Peel and slice the water chestnuts. Slice the sugar cane and section the celery.
* Heat a saucepan over medium heat and bring the oil to the boil. Saute the ginger until pungent. Shallow fry both sides of the fish bones until golden brown. Sizzle the wine and add the remaining ingredients. Stir fry until aromatic. Pour in the water and bring to the boil.
* Turn to low heat, cover with a lid and simmer for 2 hours. Add the seasoning to taste. Turn off the heat and filter the Fish Stock into a large bowl through a piece of cheese cloth. Leave to cool and store in plastic containers, marking the date of production on each. Defrost before use.

Usage:
* Fish Stock is used for making seafood dishes such as Baked Fish Rolls in White Sauce, Prawn Balls in White Sauce, and Seafood Chowder. It also serves as a soup base for Chinese Hot Pot.

材料：
魚骨2磅（1公斤）
馬蹄6安士（168克）
蔗6安士（168克）
芹菜6安士（168克）
油3湯匙
薑4片
紹酒2湯匙
胡椒粒3湯匙
水16杯

調味：
鹽2茶匙
雞精2粒

製成品：
10杯

貯存期：
雪櫃3天
冰箱2月

製法：
* 魚骨洗淨抹乾，馬蹄去皮切片，蔗切片，芹菜切段。
* 鍋燒熱，加油煮沸，爆香薑片，放下魚骨煎至兩面金黃色，灒酒，加入其餘材料爆炒至香味四溢時，注入水煮沸。
* 蓋上鍋蓋，轉用文火熬2小時，加調味料，試至合味，停火以篩加紗布過濾，晾凍，以膠杯盛起，並標明日期放於冰箱內，每次用時預先解凍。

用途：
* 此上湯宜用以烹製海鮮如白汁焗魚卷、白汁蝦球、白汁海鮮羹等，亦可用以作火鍋湯底。

註：馬蹄=荸薺

Geoduck and Watercress in Soup

上湯西菜象拔蚌

上湯西菜象拔蚌

Ingredients:

6 oz (168g) geoduck (or large clams)
6 oz (168g) watercress
1 piece bean curd
2 slices ginger
2 tbsp oil
1 tbsp wine
3 cups Fish Stock (P.47)

Seasoning:

1/4 tsp salt
1/2 tsp sugar
1/4 tsp pepper
1 tsp sesame oil

Method:

* Slice the geoduck into large thin pieces. Wash and trim the watercress. Thickly slice the bean curd and mash the ginger.

* Heat a wok over high heat and bring the oil to the boil. Saute the ginger until fragrant. Pour in the wine and the Fish Stock and return to the boil. Slide in the bean curd slices and add the watercress. Season to taste and pour in the geoduck. Return to the boil and turn off the heat. Drop in the sesame oil and serve hot.

材料：

象拔蚌6安士（168克）
西洋菜6安士（168克）
豆腐1件
薑2片
油2湯匙
酒1湯匙
魚上湯3杯（第47頁）

調味：

鹽1/4茶匙
糖1/2茶匙
胡椒粉1/4茶匙
蔴油1茶匙

製法：

* 象拔蚌切成薄片，西洋菜洗淨滴妥，豆腐分切數片，薑略拍鬆。

* 燒紅鑊，將油倒入煮沸，爆香薑片後，灒酒，加上湯煮沸，加入豆腐及西洋菜，調妥味後加象拔蚌，煮至重沸時停火，灑蔴油即成。

Flavoured Meat Sauce
香肉醬

香肉醬

Ingredients:
2 tbsp sesame oil
2 tbsp minced ginger
2 tbsp minced garlic
2 tbsp yellow wine
1 cup Stock (P.101)
1 cup fermented red bean curd
3/4 cup fermented bean curd
1/4 cup ground bean paste
1 tbsp light soy
1 chicken cube
1/2 cup sugar
2 green leeks (sectioned)

Finished Product:
3 cups

Storage Time:
1 week at room temperature
3 months in a refrigerator

Method:
* Bring the sesame oil to the boil in a wok and saute the ginger and garlic until aromatic. Sizzle the wine, then pour in the Stock and bring to the boil.
* Place the fermented red bean curd and the fermented bean curd in a bowl and mix them thoroughly with the ground bean paste, light soy, chicken cube and sugar. Pour the mixture into the wok and bring it to the boil. Adjust the flavour to taste and set aside to cool. Store in a jar and scatter in the leeks before use.

Usage:
* Besides use with stewed lamb, this tasty and fragrant sauce can also be used with other stews, such as brisket and chicken thighs. This sauce produces an aromatic smell during cooking. To increase the fragrance of meat, this sauce can be used.

材料：
蔴油2湯匙
薑茸2湯匙
蒜茸2湯匙
紹酒2湯匙
上湯1杯（第101頁）
南乳1杯
腐乳3/4杯
柱侯醬1/4杯
生抽1湯匙
雞精1粒
糖1/2杯
青蒜段2棵（後下）

製成品：
3杯

貯存期：
室溫1周
雪櫃3月

製法：
* 蔴油煮沸，將薑、蒜茸爆香，隨把紹酒灒下，加上湯煮沸。
* 南乳、腐乳、柱侯醬、生抽、雞精與糖混和，傾入上湯內拌勻重煮，調至合味，即可晾凍入瓶。煮時方可加青蒜段。

用途：
* 此醬適宜配紅燒羊肉，亦可與其他肉類如牛腩、雞腿等同燜。煮時氣味芳香，味道濃郁，烹調任何肉類如欲達致芬芳美味而齒頰留香者，皆可選用此醬。

註：南乳=紅腐乳

Lamb Stew in Flavoured Meat Sauce 香醬羊腩煲

香醬羊腩煲

Ingredients:
2 lb (1kg) lamb
4 leeks
1 sq. inch (2.5 sq.cm) old tangerine peel
1 head lettuce
16 water chestnuts
4 oz (112g) bean curd sticks
4 oz (112g) ginger
2 shallots
2 cloves garlic
1 cup Flavoured Meat Sauce (P.51)
2 tbsp Fermented Red Bean Curd Sauce (P.43)

Seasoning:
1 tbsp wine
4 cups Stock (P.101)
1 tbsp light soy
1 tsp sugar

Method:

* Wash and chop the lamb into chunks. Blanch, refresh and drain. Parch in a hot wok until dry.
* Section the leeks. Soak and shred the tangerine peel. Wash and drain the lettuce. Peel and halve the water chestnuts. Deep fry the bean curd sticks until crisp and golden then soak in water until soft. Section into 1 1/2 " (4 cm) lengths.
* Slice the ginger and mash together with the shallots and garlic.
* Heat an earthen pot with 2 tbsp oil. Saute the ginger, shallots, garlic and Flavoured Meat Sauce until fragrant. Pour in the lamb chunks and leeks and saute for 1 minute. Sizzle the wine, pour in the Stock and seasoning, and bring to the boil. Add the tangerine peel, bean curd sticks and water chestnuts. Simmer over low heat for 2 hours. Adjust the flavour to taste and serve with the Fermented Red Bean Curd Sauce. Add the lettuce before serving.

材料：
羊肉2磅（1公斤）
生蒜4條
陳皮1方吋
生菜1棵
馬蹄16粒
枝竹4安士（112克）
薑4安士（112克）
葱頭2粒
蒜頭2粒
香肉醬1杯（第51頁）
南乳香汁2湯匙（第43頁）

調味：
酒1湯匙
上湯4杯（第101頁）
生抽1湯匙
糖1茶匙

製法：

* 羊肉洗淨斬件，置沸水中略煮，取出洗淨，隔乾水分，傾入燒紅、無油的鑊內烘乾。
* 生蒜切段，陳皮浸透切絲，生菜洗淨隔乾，馬蹄去皮切開兩半。枝竹放入沸油中炸至金黃色，盛起浸於水中至軟，切成小段候用。
* 薑切片，與葱、蒜頭拍扁。
* 燒紅鍋，加油2湯匙煮沸，爆香薑、葱、蒜及香肉醬，加入羊肉、生蒜爆炒1分鐘，濽酒，加上湯及調味料煮沸，再加入果皮、枝竹及馬蹄，慢火燜2小時，試妥味，原鍋跟南乳香汁上桌，食時加生菜。

註：生菜=萵苣葉　枝竹=乾腐衣　馬蹄=荸薺

Hot Pot Dip
火鍋點食汁

火鍋點食汁

Ingredients:
1 cup light soy
1/4 cup sesame paste
1/2 cup satay paste
1 tsp chicken powder
1/2 cup sugar
1 tbsp sesame oil
1/4 tsp pepper
2 tbsp lemon juice
Serving Ingredients:
1/4 cup minced parsley
1/4 cup diced spring onion
2 tbsp parched sesame seeds
4 beaten raw eggs
Finished Product:
2 1/2 cups
Storage Time:
3 days at room temperature
1 week in a refrigerator
Method:
* Whisk the light soy, sesame paste, satay paste, chicken powder, sugar and sesame oil together in a mixing bowl while gradually adding the pepper and lemon juice. Stir evenly and adjust the flavour to taste. Store the base sauce in a jar.
Usage:
* Without the serving ingredients, Hot Pot Dip can be used as a marinade.
* Before use as a dip, add all the serving ingredients to the base sauce and mix thoroughly. Pour the dip into small serving bowls.

材料：
生抽1杯
蔴醬1/4杯
沙爹醬1/2杯
鷄粉1茶匙
糖1/2杯
蔴油1湯匙
胡椒粉1/4茶匙
檸檬汁2湯匙
後加料：
芫荽茸1/4杯
葱粒1/4杯
炒香芝蔴2湯匙
鷄蛋4隻
製成品：
2 1/2杯
貯存期：
室溫3天
雪櫃1周
製法：
* 生抽、蔴醬、沙爹、鷄粉、糖、蔴油同放桶中以蛋拂打勻，慢慢加入胡椒粉及檸檬汁和勻，試至合味。以瓶盛起隨時取用。
用途：
* 此汁除可作點食汁外，亦可用作醃料。食前方把芫荽、葱、芝蔴及鷄蛋拌入醬內，分盛小碗中。

Seafood Hot Pot
海鮮火鍋

海鮮火鍋

Ingredients:
6 oz (168g) grass carp fillet
4 oz (112g) geoduck
6 oz (168g) squid
6 oz (168g) cuttlefish balls
4 oz (112g) scallops
6 oz (168g) dace balls
10 oz (280g) snow pea sprouts
6 oz (168g) green leek
10 oz (280g) Chinese lettuce
4 oz (112g) fresh Chinese mushrooms
4 oz (112g) konjac threads
2 tbsp minced parsley
2 tbsp minced spring onion
2 tbsp parched sesame seeds
4 eggs

Soup Base:
6 cups Stock (P.101)
1/2 cup satay paste
6 oz (168g) soya bean sprouts

Condiment:
1 1/2 cups Hot Pot Dip (P.55)

Method:
* Slice the grass carp fillet and geoduck into large pieces and arrange on 2 separate platters.
* Gut and clean the squid and place on another platter.
* Place the cuttlefish balls, scallops and dace balls on 3 separate platters.
* Wash, drain and arrange the snow pea sprouts, green leek, Chinese lettuce and fresh Chinese mushrooms on different platters.
* Blanch the konjac threads in boiling salted water for 1 minute and place on a platter.
* To make the soup base, pour the Stock and satay paste into a hot pot and bring to the boil. Add the soya bean sprouts and simmer for 10 minutes.
* Blanch all the ingredients in the soup separately. Arrange the cooked ingredients back on the separate platters.
* Pour equal portions of the Hot Pot Dip in 4 small serving bowls. Crack 1 raw egg into each bowl, add the minced parsley and the diced spring onion and sesame seeds. Whisk with a pair of chopsticks or a fork until all the ingredients are evenly mixed. Serve the above cooked ingredients with this dip.

材料：
鯇魚肉6安士（168克）
象拔蚌4安士（112克）
鮮魷筒6安士（168克）
墨魚丸6安士（168克）
帶子4安士（112克）
鯪魚球6安士（168克）
豆苗10安士（280克）
韮菜6安士（168克）
唐生菜10安士（280克）
鮮冬菇4安士（112克）
魔芋絲4安士（112克）
芫荽茸2湯匙
葱茸2湯匙
炒香芝麻2湯匙
鷄蛋4隻

湯底：
上湯6杯（第101頁）
沙爹醬1/2杯
大豆芽6安士（168克）

蘸汁：
火鍋點食汁1 1/2杯（第55頁）

製法：
* 鯇魚肉及象拔蚌切成薄片，各排一碟。
* 鮮魷去內臟及頭，原隻排在另一碟中。
* 墨魚丸、帶子及鯪魚球各排一碟。
* 豆苗、韮菜、唐生菜及鮮冬菇洗淨，隔乾水分，排妥。
* 魔芋絲以沸鹽水灼1分鐘，將全部材料排妥於桌上。
* 上湯、沙爹醬傾入火鍋內煮沸，再加入大豆芽煮10分鐘。
* 將各海鮮材料分別放鍋中灼熟，分放回碟上。
* 火鍋汁分置於4個小碗中，加入芫荽、葱茸及芝蔴，拌入鷄蛋拌勻，即可把灼熟海鮮放入蘸食。

註：鯇魚=草魚　生菜=萵苣葉　冬菇=香菇

Lime and Fishsoy Sauce
青檸魚露汁

青檸魚露汁

Ingredients:
1/4 cup peeled garlic
4 red chillies
1/2 cup lime juice (or vinegar)
1/3 cup sugar
1 cup fishsoy
1/4 cup Stock (P.101)

Finished Product:
2 cups

Storage Time:
1 month at room temperature
4 months in a refrigerator

Method:
* Mince the garlic and chillies into a puree using a food processor. Remove into a large bowl, pour in the lime juice and stir in the sugar until it dissolves.
* Mix the fishsoy and Stock in another bowl and stream the mixture in the garlic puree. Blend the ingredients thoroughly. Season to taste then store in an air-tight jar for future use.

Usage:
* Apart from using this sauce as a gravy for pork chop, it also goes well as a dip for Vietnamese Spring Rolls and Vietnamese Vermicelli.

材料：
蒜肉1/4杯
紅椒4隻
青檸汁或白醋1/2杯
糖1/3杯
魚露1杯
上湯1/4杯（第101頁）

製成品：
2杯

貯存期：
室溫1月
雪櫃4月

製法：
* 蒜頭、紅椒同放碎肉機中攪爛成茸，取出放大碗內，加醋或檸汁拌勻後，將糖傾入拌溶。
* 魚露與上湯放另一碗中和勻，加入醋中攪拌，試妥味後入瓶。

用途：
* 此汁除用於豬扒上，亦可與越南春卷及潻粉伴食。

註：魚露=蝦油　豬扒=豬排

Pork Chops in Lime Fishsoy Sauce
魚露豬扒

魚露豬扒

Ingredients:
8 oz (224g) pork chop
2 shallots
10 cloves garlic
1 sprig lemon grass
2 tbsp oil
4 blanched baby carrot
3 blanched broccoli florets
4 tbsp Lime and Fishsoy Sauce (P.59)
1 tbsp minced mint
2 tbsp chopped chilli

Meat Marinade:
1 tsp fishsoy
2 tbsp lemon grass juice
2 tsp sugar
1/4 tsp pepper

Method:
* Cut the pork chop into 1/2 inch (1.2cm) thick pieces. Pat them lightly with the blade of a meat cleaver.
* Mince the shallots and garlic. Chop the lemon grass finely. Blend in all the meat marinade ingredients. Season to taste. Immerse the pork chop slices and soak for 10 minutes.
* Heat a wok and bring the oil to the boil. Sear each side of the pork slices for 3 minutes until golden brown. Remove on to a platter. Arrange the carrot and broccoli round the pork. Pour the Lime and Fishsoy Sauce on top and garnish with the minced mint and chilli.

材料：
豬扒8安士（224克）
蒜頭2粒
葱頭10粒
香茅1枝
油2湯匙
熟紅蘿蔔4條
熟西蘭花3小棵
青檸魚露汁4湯匙（第59頁）
香花菜茸1湯匙
紅椒圈 2 湯匙

醃料：
魚露1茶匙
香茅汁2湯匙
糖2茶匙
胡椒粉1/4茶匙

製法：
* 豬扒切約1/2吋（1.2公分）厚塊，用刀背或鬆肉器底面拍鬆。
* 蒜頭及葱頭剁茸，香茅切碎，與醃料和勻，將豬扒放入醃10分鐘。
* 煎鑊燒熱，加油煮沸，把豬扒放入鑊中，以文火煎3分鐘，反轉煎3分鐘，盛起，與熟紅蘿蔔及西蘭花排放碟上，將青檸魚露汁淋下，再灑香花菜茸及紅椒圈即可上桌。

註：豬扒=豬排

Onion Garlic Sauce
洋葱蒜茸汁

洋葱蒜茸汁

Ingredients:
4 oz (112g) garlic
2 oz (56g) onion
1 oz (28g) butter
2 1/4 cups Stock (P.101)
1/4 tsp salt
1/2 tsp sugar
1/4 tsp pepper

Finished Product:
2 cups

Storage Time:
1 month in a refrigerator
3 months in a freezer

Method:
* Mince the garlic and finely dice the onion.
* Melt the butter in a frying pan. Saute the garlic and onion until fragrant. Stir in the Stock and simmer for 2 minutes. Add the salt, sugar and pepper. Filter the mixture through a fine sieve and set aside to cool. Store in a jar.

Usage:
* This sauce is best mixed with macaroni, spaghetti, or served as a gravy for pork chop or seafood.

材料：
蒜頭4安士（112克）
洋葱2 安士（56克）
牛油1安士（28克）
上湯2 1/4杯（第101頁）
鹽1/4茶匙
糖1/2茶匙
胡椒粉1/4茶匙

製成品：
2杯

貯存期：
雪櫃1月
冰箱3月

製法：
* 蒜頭剁茸，洋葱切碎。
* 煎鍋燒熱，放入牛油煮溶，加入洋葱及蒜茸炒透，再傾入上湯煮2分鐘，加鹽、糖及胡椒粉調味後，隔去渣，晾凍後即可入瓶。
* 洋葱蒜茸汁宜配以意大利粉、通粉伴食。亦可用作豬扒或海鮮之汁液。

Pasta with Onion Garlic Sauce
蒜茸煙肉蜆殼粉

蒜茸煙肉蜆殼粉

Ingredients:

8 oz (224g) pasta shells
4 cups water
1 tbsp salt
2 tbsp butter
2 oz (56g) bacon
1 cup oil
1 cup Onion Garlic Sauce (P.63)
1 tbsp minced parsley

Method:

* Place the pasta shells in a saucepan. Add the water and salt and bring to the boil. Continue to cook for 6 minutes, then turn off the heat. Set aside for 8 minutes, and drain.
* Melt the butter in a frying pan. Pour in the pasta shells and stir fry, then remove on to a dish.
* Dice the bacon. Clean the frying pan, pour in the oil and bring it to the boil. Deep fry the bacon until crisp. Drain off the excess oil.
* Reheat the frying pan over medium heat, add the Garlic Onion Sauce and bring it to the boil. Pour in the pasta shells, mix well with the sauce and turn off the heat. Remove on to a platter, scatter the minced parsley and crispy bacon on top.

材料：

蜆殼粉8安士（224克）
水4杯
鹽1湯匙
牛油2湯匙
煙肉2安士（56克）
油1杯
洋葱蒜茸汁1杯（第63頁）
番芫荽茸1湯匙

製法：

* 蜆殼粉傾在厚深鍋內加水及鹽煮沸，續煮6分鐘，熄火浸8分鐘後取出，將多餘水分隔去。
* 煎鍋燒熱，放入牛油煮溶，將蜆殼粉傾下炒勻（約1分鐘），盛在碟上。
* 煙肉切碎後將油煮沸，放下煙肉茸炸至香脆。將油倒起留用。
* 煎鍋燒熱，傾下蒜茸洋葱汁煮沸，將蜆殼粉倒入，停火拌勻上碟。灑下番芫荽及煙肉茸即可上桌熱食。

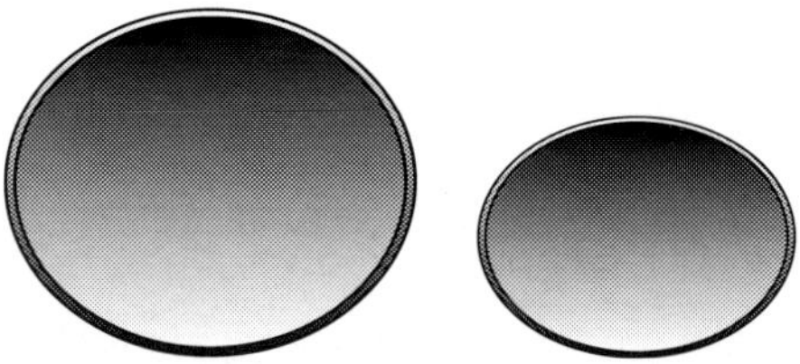

Prawn Stock
蝦上湯

蝦上湯

Ingredients:
2 lb (1 kg) prawn heads and shells
4 oz (112g) water chestnut
4 oz (112g) carrot
4 oz (112g) sugar cane
4 oz (112g) celery
3 tbsp oil
2 slices ginger
4 shallots
1 tbsp peppercorn
2 tbsp yellow wine
16 cups water
Seasoning:
1 tbsp salt
1 chicken cube
Finished Product:
6 cups
Storage Time:
3 days in a refrigerator
1 month in a freezer
Method:
* Wash and drain the prawn heads and shells. Peel and slice the water chestnut and carrot. Slice the sugar cane. Section the celery.
* Heat a saucepan over high heat and bring the oil to the boil. Saute the ginger, shallots and peppercorn until pungent. Stir fry the prawn heads and shells until fragrant. Add the water chestnut, carrot, sugar cane and celery. Pour in the yellow wine and the water and bring to the boil.
* Cover the saucepan with a lid and simmer for 2 hours over low heat. Stir in the salt and the chicken cube until both dissolve. Adjust the flavour to taste.Turn off the heat. Place a piece of muslin over a sieve and filter the broth into a large bowl. Leave to cool. Store the prawn broth in 8 fl oz (1 cup) air-tight plastic containers, marking the date of production on each. They can be kept in the freezer and defrosted before use.
Usage:
* Prawn Stock is used as a base for cooking sauces for seafood such as King Prawn Sauce and Large Mussel Sauce. It is also used as a base for Won Ton Soup.

材料：
蝦殼2磅（1公斤）
馬蹄4安士（112克）
紅蘿蔔4安士（112克）
蔗4安士（112克）
芹菜4安士（112克）
油3湯匙
薑2片
葱頭4粒
胡椒粒1湯匙
紹酒2湯匙
水16杯
調味：
鹽1湯匙
鷄精1粒
製成品：
6杯
貯存期：
雪櫃3天
冰箱1月
製法：
＊　蝦殼洗淨，隔乾水分，馬蹄與紅蘿蔔去皮切片，蔗切片，芹菜切段。
＊　鍋燒熱，加油煮沸，爆香薑片、葱頭、胡椒粒，倒下蝦殼炒透至香味四溢時，即把馬蹄、紅蘿蔔、蔗及芹菜傾下，灒酒，加水煮沸。
＊　蓋上鍋蓋，轉用文火熬2小時，加鹽及鷄精調至合味，停火，以篩加紗布過濾，晾凍，以8安士（1杯）膠杯分別盛載，並標明日期，排放於冰箱內，每次取用時預先解凍。
用途：
＊　此上湯宜用以烹製海產配汁，如大蝦汁、青蠔配汁等，也可作雲吞湯底。
註：馬蹄＝荸薺　雲吞＝餛飩

Leek and Shrimp Won Ton
韮菜雲吞

韮菜雲吞

Ingredients:
5 oz (140g) peeled fresh shrimps
2 oz (56g) green leek
6 oz (168g) won ton pastry
1/2 beaten eggwhite
1/2 wok water
2 tbsp oil
1 slice ginger
1 shallot
8 oz (224g) soya bean sprouts
1 tbsp diced spring onion
Marinade:
1/4 tsp salt
1/2 tsp sugar
1 tsp cornflour
1/4 tsp pepper
1/2 eggwhite
1/2 tsp sesame oil
Seasoning:
1 tsp wine
4 cups Prawn Stock (P.67)
1/2 tsp salt
1 chicken cube
1/4 tsp pepper
1 tsp sesame oil
Method:
* Peel, wash, dry and coarsely dice the fresh shrimps. Mix them thoroughly with the marinade ingredients and leave for 10 minutes. Dice the green leek and mix it with 1/2 tbsp oil. Blend the shrimps with the leek in a bowl and pound the mixture until firm to make the filling.
* Place 1 tsp filling on a corner of the won ton pastry. Roll it up, folding in either side, and seal the won ton with the beaten eggwhite.
* Bring the water to the boil in a wok over high heat and carefully slide in all the won ton. Turn to medium heat and simmer until the won ton float on the surface. Drain and place the won ton in a large serving bowl.
* Reheat the wok and bring the oil to the boil. Saute the ginger and shallot until aromatic and discard them. Pour in the soya bean sprouts and stir fry for 2 minutes. Sizzle the wine, add the Prawn Stock and simmer over low heat for 1 hour. Filter the stock through a sieve into a saucepan. Stir in the salt, chicken cube and pepper until dissolved. Pour this soup on the won ton in the serving bowl. Sprinkle the sesame oil and diced spring onion on top and serve immediately.

材料：
蝦肉5安士（140克）
韮菜2安士（56克）
雲吞皮6安士（168克）
蛋白1/2隻
沸水1/2鍋
油2湯匙
薑1片
葱頭1粒
大豆芽8安士（224克）
葱粒1湯匙
醃料：
鹽1/4茶匙
糖1/2茶匙
生粉1茶匙
胡椒粉1/4茶匙
鷄蛋白1/2隻
蔴油1/2茶匙
調味：
酒1茶匙
蝦上湯4杯（第67頁）
鹽1/2茶匙
鷄精1粒
胡椒粉1/4茶匙
蔴油1茶匙
製法：
* 蝦肉洗淨抹乾切粗粒，用混合醃料拌匀醃10分鐘。韮菜切粒，用油1/2湯匙拌匀後與醃妥之蝦混和，用手攪匀略撻。
* 雲吞皮攤開，每張放入餡料約1茶匙，包妥，以蛋白收口。
* 將雲吞放入沸水中煮至浮起時（約6分鐘），盛起放於大碗中。
* 燒紅鑊，加油爆香薑片、葱頭後棄去，傾入大豆芽炒透，灒酒，加上湯煮沸，改用文火續煮1小時，隔去豆芽，調妥味後即將上湯倒於雲吞上，灑蔴油、葱粒，上桌熱食。

註：雲吞=餛飩

Red Wine Sauce
紅酒汁

紅酒汁

Ingredients:
2 oz (56g) onion
2 oz (56g) carrot
1 oz (28g) celery
2 tbsp oil
1/4 cup tomato puree
2 cups red wine
2 cups Stock (P.101) or Prawn Stock (P.67)
2 oz (56g) butter
1/2 tsp salt
1/2 tsp black pepper
1/2 cup White Sauce (see Roux P.79)
1/2 cup fresh cream

Finished Product:
3 cups

Storage Time:
1 week in a refrigerator
1 month in a freezer

Method:
* Dice the onion, carrot and celery. Heat a saucepan and bring the oil to the boil. Saute the onion, carrot and celery until aromatic. Add the tomato puree and sizzle in the red wine. Simmer until the mixture reboils. Pour in the Stock and simmer over low heat for 1 hour, reducing the stock to only 3 cups. Filter the stock into a large bowl through a piece of cheese cloth. Add the butter, salt and black pepper and mix thoroughly. Blend in the White Sauce and fresh cream before use.

Usage:
* Red Wine Sauce is used for stewing chicken or as a gravy for lobster and chicken fillet. It also goes with fish or meat.

材料：
洋葱2安士（56克）
紅蘿蔔2安士（56克）
西芹1安士（28克）
油2湯匙
茄膏1/4杯
紅酒2杯
上湯或蝦湯2杯（第101頁／第67頁）
牛油2安士（56克）
鹽1/2茶匙
黑胡椒粉1/2茶匙
白汁1/2杯（第79頁）
奶油1/2杯

製成品：
3杯

貯存期：
雪櫃1周
冰箱1月

製法：
* 洋葱、紅蘿蔔、西芹切粒，將油煮沸，將上述材料爆香後，加入茄膏拌匀。瀆下紅酒煮沸，即把蝦湯傾入，以文火續煮1小時，待濃縮至只餘3杯，以紗布過濾後，即將牛油拌入和匀，加鹽及黑椒粉試至合味，使用前加入白汁及奶油拌匀，即成紅酒汁。

用途：
* 紅酒汁香滑可口，除可用以扒龍蝦、燴鷄及淋在鷄扒上之外，尚可與其他魚或肉類配合。

註：西芹＝洋芹

Pigeon in Red Wine Sauce
紅酒焗乳鴿

紅酒焗乳鴿

Ingredients:

1 pigeon
1 tbsp ginger juice
1 tbsp red wine
2 tbsp dark soy
2 slices ginger
2 shallots
1 spring onion
2 tbsp oil
1 cup Red Wine Sauce (P.71)
2 tbsp White Sauce (see Roux P.79)
2 tbsp fresh cream

Seasoning:

1/4 tsp salt
1 tsp light soy
1/2 chicken cube
1/4 tsp pepper

Method:

* Wash and dry the pigeon. Brush the inside and outside of the whole bird with the ginger juice and red wine. Set aside to dry for 20 minutes. Brush thoroughly with the dark soy.

* Mash the ginger and shallots. Shred the spring onion.

* Heat a saucepan over medium heat and bring the oil to the boil. Saute the ginger and shallots until aromatic. Add the pigeon and shallow fry it until golden brown. Sizzle in the Red Wine Sauce and seasoning. Cover with a lid and cook for 15 minutes. Turn over and cook the other side for 15 minutes. Remove and cut into serving pieces. Arrange on a platter. Reboil the Red Wine Sauce, stir in the White Sauce and fresh cream and mix evenly. Pour the mixture over the pigeon pieces and sprinkle the spring onion on top.

材料：

乳鴿1隻
薑汁1湯匙
紅酒1湯匙
老抽2湯匙
薑2片
葱頭2粒
葱1棵
油2湯匙
紅酒汁1杯（第71頁）
白汁2湯匙（第79頁）
奶油2湯匙

調味：

鹽1/4茶匙
生抽1茶匙
鷄精1/2粒
胡椒粉1/4茶匙

製法

* 乳鴿洗淨抹乾，以薑汁及紅酒塗勻鴿身內外，放置一旁吹20分鐘，塗上老抽。

* 薑、葱頭拍扁，葱切細絲。

* 鍋燒熱，加油煮沸，放入薑、葱頭爆香，將鴿放入煎至全身金黃色，隨把紅酒汁濺下，加調味料拌勻，蓋密焗15分鐘，揭蓋轉身再焗15分鐘。取出斬件上碟排妥，把汁煮至重沸，將白汁、奶油拌入和勻，淋在乳鴿上，灑葱絲上桌。

Rose Wine Soy Sauce
玫瑰豉油汁

玫瑰豉油汁

Ingredients:
3 slices ginger
3 shallots
3 cups spicy sauce
6 cups dark soy
10-12 oz (280-336g) rock sugar
1/2 cup rose wine

Finished Product:
10 cups

Storage Time:
1 year in a refrigerator
Several years in a freezer

Method:
* Mash the ginger and shallots.
* Pour the spicy sauce and dark soy into a deep saucepan. Add the rock sugar, ginger and shallots and bring to the boil. Turn off the heat and add in the rose wine. Season to taste.
* Leave the Rose Wine Soy Sauce to cool. Pour into a clean plastic container with the date marked on it. Store in a refrigerator or freezer. If stored in a refrigerator, the sauce should be reboiled monthly for best results.

Usage:
* The sauce is generally used for poaching pigeon and chicken, but can also be served as a marinade or a dip.

材料：
薑3片
葱頭3粒
鹵水3杯
老抽6杯
冰糖10至12安士（280克至336克）
玫瑰露1/2杯

製成品：
10杯

貯存期：
雪櫃1年
冰箱數年

製法：
* 薑及葱頭拍扁。
* 鹵水及老抽同放深鍋中，加糖、薑及葱頭煮沸，停火加入玫瑰露，試妥味即成。
* 玫瑰豉油汁晾凍後，傾入清潔乾爽之膠盒中，標明製造日期，置雪櫃或冰箱中貯存。若放雪櫃內最好每月煮沸一次。

用途：
* 此豉油汁除可用以浸製豉油乳鴿、豉油鷄等外，也可作醃料或蘸汁，用途廣泛。

Pigeons in Soy Sauce
豉油雙鴿

豉油雙鴿

Ingredients:

2 pigeons, 1 lb (1/2 kg) each
2 tbsp coarse sea salt
1/2 wok water
10 cups Rose Wine Soy Sauce (P.75)
2 tsp sesame oil

Method:

* Rub the pigeons with the salt. Remove the giblets and rinse the pigeons thoroughly.

* Bring the water to the boil in a wok, poach the pigeons for about 1/2 minute until the skins tighten.Rinse and hang them up to dry.

* Pour the Rose Wine Soy Sauce into a saucepan and bring it to the boil. Add the pigeons and cover tightly with a lid. When the sauce is boiling, turn off the heat and leave the pigeons in the saucepan to soak for 18 minutes. Remove and brush with sesame oil. Chop the pigeons into bite-sized pieces and arrange on a platter. Pour 3 tbsp Rose Wine Soy Sauce over the birds and serve.

材料：

乳鴿2隻共2磅（1公斤）
粗鹽2湯匙
水1/2鍋
玫瑰豉油汁10杯（第75頁）
蔴油2茶匙

製法：

* 乳鴿用鹽擦去污迹，去內臟後再洗淨。

* 水煮沸，將鴿放入浸1/2分鐘至皮收縮，取出清洗後吊乾水分。

* 玫瑰豉油汁放鍋中煮沸，將鴿放入，蓋密，煮至重沸時。停火浸18分鐘，取出塗上蔴油，斬件排在碟上，淋下3湯匙玫瑰豉油汁在鴿上即成。

Roux 白汁麪撈

白汁麪撈

Ingredients:
4 oz (112g) butter
8 oz (224g) plain flour
1/2 cup fresh milk
Finished Product
1 lb (1/2 kg)
Storage Time:
3 days in a refrigerator
1 month in a freezer
Method:
* Melt the butter in a small saucepan over moderate heat.
* Turn off the heat and sieve in the flour. Stir with a wooden spoon until the flour and butter are well blended.
* Slowly stream in the fresh milk. Turn on the heat and stir until the sauce thickens and a dough (Roux) is formed. Continue to cook for 30 seconds until the Roux is soft and thoroughly cooked. Remove and leave to cool. Store in a refrigerator or freezer.
Usage:
* **Baking Sauce -** Heat 1 1/2 cups Stock and 1/2 cup fresh milk in a double-boiler. Put 4 oz (112g) Roux in a small saucepan. Using low heat, slowly stream the hot liquid over the Roux and stir evenly. Blend in salt and pepper and stir until the sauce thickens. Filter through a sieve and pour over the dish to be baked.
* **White Sauce -** Heat and stir 2 1/2 cups Stock and 1/2 cup fresh milk with 4 oz (112g) Roux in a saucepan over low heat. Add salt, pepper and season to taste. Filter through a sieve and serve as a runny sauce for seafood dishes.
* **Curry Sauce -** Add 3 tbsp curry powder to 1 1/2 cups White Sauce.
* **Mustard Sauce -** Add 3 tbsp mustard to 1 1/2 cups White Sauce.
* **Parsley Sauce -** Add 1/2 cup chopped hard-boiled egg and 2 tbsp minced parsley to 1 1/2 cups White Sauce and stir thoroughly.

材料：
牛油4安士（112克）
麪粉8安士（224克）
鮮奶1/2杯
製成品：
1磅（1/2公斤）
貯存期：
雪櫃3天
冰箱1月
製法：
* 小鍋1隻放爐上以文火燒熱，放入牛油煮溶。
* 停火將麪粉篩入，以木棍拌攪至均勻。
* 鮮奶慢慢流入鍋中，不斷把麪粉攪拌。然後重開火，將白汁邊煮邊攪至汁轉濃而成一麪糰（此即為麪撈）。續煮約 1/2分鐘至麪粉全熟，而麪撈軟滑無粒，即可盛起，貯藏於冰箱，隨時取用。
用途：
* **焗菜濃汁**一將上湯1 1/2杯與鮮奶1/2杯坐熱後，把4安士（112克）麪撈放於小鍋中，將熱流質逐少傾入，以文火拌勻，加鹽、胡椒粉煮濃，隔去小粒，即成一種蓋面用之焗菜濃汁。
* **海鮮菜獻汁**一將上湯2 1/2杯與鮮奶1/2杯混和坐熱後，把4安士（112克）凍麪撈放小鍋中，將熱流質逐少傾入拌勻，加鹽、胡椒粉煮稀，隔去小粒，即成一種淋於海鮮上之稀白汁獻。
* **咖喱汁**一加入咖喱粉3湯匙於1 1/2杯稀白汁中拌勻，即成咖喱汁。
* **芥辣汁**一加入芥醬3湯匙於1 1/2杯稀白汁中拌勻，即成芥辣汁。
* **芫荽鷄蛋汁**一加入切碎熟鷄蛋1/2杯及芫荽茸2湯匙於1 1/2杯稀白汁中，即成芫荽鷄蛋汁。

芫荽汁鮑魚卷

Ingredients:

1 tin abalone
12 asparagus tips
12 celery threads
1 1/2 cups Stock (P.101)
1 tbsp oil
2 oz (56g) Roux (P.79)
1 1/2 cups Fish Stock (P.47)
1 tsp white wine
1/4 tsp pepper
1/4 tsp salt
3 tbsp minced parsley

Method:

* Thinly slice the abalone into large pieces. Wash the asparagus and blanch it in the Stock with the oil for 1 minute. Add the celery threads and soak for 10 seconds. Drain and rinse under a running tap.

* Place the sliced abalone on the table and put an asparagus tip on one end of the abalone. Roll it up and tie with a celery thread. Arrange on a platter.

* Place the Roux in a saucepan, add the hot Fish Stock and stir thoroughly. Bring the mixture to the boil over low heat. Drop in the wine and the minced parsley. Season to taste and arrange the abalone rolls in the parsley sauce. Cook for 30 seconds and dish.

Tips:

* The tinned abalone used for this dish is already cooked. If fresh abalone is used, it should be cooked in advance over low heat for 3 to 4 hours until soft.

* Ideally, pencil-thin asparagus should be used. Thicker asparagus should be sliced lengthwise into halves before use.

* If abalone is too expensive, thinly sliced garoupa meat can be used as a substitute. The garoupa should be marinated with ginger juice and pepper before use.

*The cooking time for garoupa rolls should be extended to 2 minutes.

材料：

罐頭鮑魚1罐
露筍尖12條
芹菜絲12條
上湯1 1/2杯（第101頁）
油1湯匙
麪撈2安士（56克）（第79頁）
魚上湯1 1/2杯（第47頁）
白酒1茶匙
胡椒粉1/4茶匙
鹽1/4茶匙
芫荽茸3湯匙

製法：

* 鮑魚切大薄片，露筍洗淨放於上湯中，加油煮1分鐘，加入芹菜絲浸片刻（大約10秒鐘），一同盛起置水喉下沖凍。

* 鮑魚片平放桌上，將露筍放入捲成筒，用芹菜紮緊，置碟中候用。

* 小鍋中放入麪撈，逐少加入沸上湯，邊拌邊以文火煮沸和成滑糊，灒酒加入芫荽茸同煮，調味後，排入鮑魚卷煮1/2分鐘，試妥味，盛在熱碟中上桌。

註：露筍=蘆筍

烹飪秘訣：

* 此菜因採用罐頭鮑魚，故毋須預先將鮑魚烹煮，若用鮮鮑代替，則須預早數小時把鮑魚文火煮至軟身方可取用。

* 用作鮑魚卷餡心之露筍必須採用似鉛筆幼身之露筍。如用粗身者，則將每條筍尖破為兩半。

* 鮑魚價格昂貴，可用石斑肉薄片代替，但必須先以薑汁、胡椒粉醃10分鐘。

* 轉用魚肉卷時，烹煮時間須延長至2分鐘。

Abalone Rolls in Parsley Sauce

芫荽汁鮑魚卷

Crab in White Sauce
奶油焗蟹

奶油焗蟹

Ingredients:
2 lb (1kg) whole crab
4 cups oil
2 oz (56g) celery
2 oz (56g) onion
2 oz (56g) green pepper
2 oz (56g) red pepper
2 slices ginger
1 shallot
1 clove garlic
1 cup White Sauce (see Roux P.79)

Seasoning:
1/2 tsp salt
1 tsp wine
1/2 cup Stock (P.101)
1/2 cup milk
1/2 tsp sugar
1/4 tsp pepper
1 tsp sesame oil

Method:
* Clean and dry the crab thoroughly and sprinkle with 2 tbsp cornflour. Pour the oil into a wok and parboil the crab over low heat until golden brown. Drain and leave 2 tbsp oil in the wok.
* Clean and dice the celery, onion, red and green peppers. Mince the ginger, shallot and garlic.
* Bring the 2 tbsp oil to the boil in a wok. Sprinkle salt and saute the minced ingredients until aromatic. Pour in the diced ingredients, toss briefly and add the crab. Sizzle the wine, then trickle in the Stock and milk. Reboil and stir in the White Sauce. Season to taste, cover the wok with a lid, and cook for a further 5 minutes. Serve with the sesame oil sprinkled on top.

材料：
肉蟹2磅（1公斤）
油4杯
西芹2安士（56克）
洋葱2安士（56克）
青椒2安士（56克）
紅椒2安士（56克）
薑2片
葱頭1粒
蒜頭1粒
白汁1杯（第79頁）

調味：
鹽1/2茶匙
酒1茶匙
上湯1/2杯（第101頁）
鮮奶1/2杯
糖1/2茶匙
胡椒粉1/4茶匙
蔴油1茶匙

製法：
* 蟹洗擦乾淨，劏開去腸臟後再沖洗一次。隔乾水分，灑上生粉約2湯匙，置熱油鍋內泡至轉色，盛起候用。
* 西芹、洋葱、青紅椒清理後切細粒。薑、葱、蒜剁茸。
* 燒紅鑊，加油2湯匙煮沸，灑鹽及加入薑、葱、蒜茸，以文火略爆。隨即加入全部細粒炒片刻。繼將蟹傾入鑊中，濽酒，加上湯及鮮奶煮沸。撥開鑊中各物，把白汁倒入拌攪成奶油，最後加調味料，試妥味，蓋上鑊蓋焗5分鐘。揭蓋加尾油上碟。

註：西芹=洋芹

Sea Cucumber Chowder
白汁海參羹

白汁海參羹

Ingredients:

4 oz (112g) baby sea cucumber
4 oz (112g) sea slug
2 slices ginger (mashed)
2 spring onions (sectioned)
1 tbsp wine
1 cup Stock (P.101)
5 oz (140g) Roux (P.79)
4 1/2 cups Fish Stock (P.47)
1/2 cup fresh cream

Seasoning:

1/4 tsp salt
1 tsp chicken powder
1/4 tsp pepper

Method:

* Slice the sea cucumber and wash the sea slug. Heat a wok with 2 tbsp oil and saute the ginger and spring onions until fragrant. Sizzle the wine, pour in the Stock and bring to the boil. Add the sea cucumber and sea slug, simmer for 20 minutes and drain.

* Place the Roux in a saucepan, gradually stir in the Fish Stock. Bring to the boil over moderate heat and stir occasionally. Drop in the sea cucumber and sea slug. Blend in the cream and add seasoning to taste. Pour into individual soup tureens and serve.

材料：

濕海參4安士（112克）
白海參4安士（112克）
薑2片（略拍）
葱2棵（切段）
酒1湯匙
上湯1杯（第101頁）
白汁麪撈5安士（140克）（第79頁）
魚上湯4 1/2杯（第47頁）
奶油1/2杯

調味：

鹽1/4茶匙
雞精1茶匙
胡椒粉1/4茶匙

製法：

* 海參切成薄片。燒紅鑊，加油2湯匙煮沸，爆香薑及葱，灒酒，加上湯煮沸，再加入兩種海參煨至入味（約20分鐘），隔乾備用。

* 麪撈放於鍋內，逐少加入魚上湯拌勻，移在中火爐上煮沸，即將兩種海參同時傾入湯中，最後拌入奶油及調味料，試至合味，倒在小湯鍋中即成。

Scallop Sauce
瑤柱汁

瑤柱汁

Ingredients:
8 oz (224g) soaked dried scallops
2 slices ginger
2 shallots
3 tbsp oil
1 tsp wine
3 cups scallop stock mixed with water
1/4 tsp salt
1/2 tsp sugar
1/4 tsp pepper
1 tbsp cornflour
1 tbsp water

Finished Product:
3 cups

Storage Time:
3 days in a refrigerator
2 months in a freezer

Method:
* Put the soaked dried scallops in a bowl, place it on a rack in a wok and steam over moderate heat for 1 hour. Remove and set aside to cool, then shred.
* Mash the ginger and shallots.
* Heat the oil in the wok and saute the ginger and shallots, then discard. Stir in the scallops and stir fry for 10 seconds. Sizzle the wine, pour in the scallop water, bring to the boil and season to taste. Leave to cool and store in a jar.
* Before using the Scallop Sauce, mix the cornflour with the water. Slowly stream the mixture into the base sauce to thicken.

Usage:
* Scallop Sauce is rich, tasty and nutritious but it takes a long time to prepare. It is quicker and more convenient to make a large quantity and store it in a refrigerator or freezer. Use a little sauce as a gravy poured over cooked vegetables to enhance the flavour of the dish.

材料：
濕瑤柱8安士（224克）
薑2片
葱頭2粒
油3湯匙
酒1茶匙
瑤柱水加水共3杯
鹽1/4茶匙
糖1/2茶匙
胡椒粉1/4茶匙
生粉1湯匙
水1湯匙

製成品：
3杯

貯存期：
雪櫃3天
冰箱2月

製法：
* 濕瑤柱放在碗中，置蒸架上以中火蒸1小時，取出晾凍，撕成細絲。
* 薑、葱頭拍扁。
* 燒紅鑊，加油爆香薑、葱頭，棄去。放入瑤柱爆炒片刻（約10秒），灒酒，傾入瑤柱水煮沸。試妥味後晾凍入瓶留用。
* 每次取用時加生粉水和成獻。

用途：
* 瑤柱汁為一種味道濃郁、美味可口而滋養之汁液，每次取用少量即可令菜式生色不少。由於蒸燉需時，故宜每次多做以備不時之需。

Winter Melon in Scallop Sauce
瑤柱瓜條

瑤柱瓜條

Ingredients:
20 oz (560g) winter melon
2 slices ginger
2 shallots
2 spring onions
2 tbsp oil
parsley to garnish

Seasoning:
1/4 tsp salt
1 tsp wine
1/2 cup Scallop Sauce (P.89)
2 tsp light soy
1 tsp sugar
1/4 tsp pepper
1 tsp cornflour
1 tsp water
1 tsp sesame oil

Method:
* Peel and cut the winter melon into finger-sized pieces. Shred the ginger and slice the shallots. Section the spring onions.
* Heat the oil in a wok and saute the salt, ginger and shallots. Stir in the winter melon and fry for 1 minute. Sizzle the wine, add the Scallop Sauce and mix well. Cover with a lid and simmer for 2 minutes. Mix the cornflour with the water. Remove the lid and stream in the mixture to thicken the sauce.
* Scatter the spring onions on top and drop in the sesame oil. Toss thoroughly and dish. Garnish with the parsley.

材料：
冬瓜20安士（560克）
薑2片
葱頭2粒
葱2棵
油2湯匙
洋芫荽（裝飾）

調味：
鹽1/4茶匙
酒1茶匙
瑤柱汁1/2杯（第89頁）
生抽2茶匙
糖1茶匙
胡椒粉1/4茶匙
生粉1茶匙
水1茶匙
蔴油1茶匙

製法：
* 冬瓜去皮切如手指條，薑切絲，葱頭切片，葱切段。
* 燒紅鑊，加油煮沸，灑鹽，爆香薑葱片，倒入冬瓜拌炒1分鐘。灒酒，加入瑤柱汁炒片刻，蓋上鑊蓋煮2分鐘，揭蓋，調妥味，以生粉加水和獻，灑葱段，淋上蔴油拌勻即成。用洋芫荽裝飾。

Simple Brown Sauce
簡易黃汁

Ingredients:
6 oz (168g) celery
6 oz (168g) carrot
6 oz (168g) onion
1/4 cup oil
1 cup plain flour
1 tin tomato puree
4 cups beef stock
4 cups water

Seasoning:
1 tsp black peppercorn
3 bay leaves
1/2 tsp salt
1/2 tbsp sugar
2 beef cubes
1 tbsp dark soy

Finished Product:
5 cups

Storage Time:
1 month in a refrigerator
3 months in a freezer

Method:
* Slice the celery, carrot and onion thinly.
* Heat a saucepan and bring the oil to the boil. Fry the celery, carrot and onion for 5 minutes. Add the flour, turn off the heat and stir thoroughly for another 10 minutes. Blend in the tomato puree. Add the beef stock and water. Turn to medium heat and simmer for 10 minutes. Stir in all the seasoning and continue to simmer for 2 hours.
* Sift the mixture into a large bowl and leave to cool. Store in an air-tight jar. Keep in a refrigerator or freezer for future use.

Usage:
* Brown Sauce is one of the basic sauces used in Western cooking. It is used as a base for Black Pepper Sauce or Mushroom Sauce to be served with beef dishes such as steaks. It is also an essential ingredient of thick soups such as Oxtail Soup and Russian Borsch, and for pasta sauces such as Spaghetti Bolognaise.

簡易黃汁

材料：
西芹6安士（168克）
紅蘿蔔6安士（168克）
洋葱6安士（168克）
油1/4杯
麪粉1杯
茄膏1罐
牛肉清湯4杯
水4杯

調味：
黑椒粒1茶匙
香葉3片
鹽1/2茶匙
糖1/2湯匙
牛精2粒
老抽1湯匙

製成品：
5杯

貯存期：
雪櫃1月
冰箱3月

製法：
* 西芹、紅蘿蔔及洋葱切大片。
* 鍋燒熱，加油煮沸，放入西芹、紅蘿蔔及洋葱炒5分鐘，再加麪粉熄火炒10分鐘，將茄膏加入同炒勻，慢慢注入牛肉清湯及水，以文火煮10分鐘，拌入調味料慢火熬約2小時。
* 黃汁煮好，隔去渣，晾凍後入瓶，放冰箱或雪櫃內留用。

用途：
* 黃汁乃西餐基本汁之一種，可用以調製各種牛柳配汁如白菌汁、黑椒汁等，亦可用於烹製濃湯如羅宋湯、牛尾湯，更可作意大利粉之基本汁。

註：西芹=洋芹

Ox-Tongue in Brown Sauce
黄汁燴牛脷

黃汁燴牛脷

Ingredients:
2 lb (1 kg) ox-tongue
6 slices ginger
3 star anises
1 tsp peppercorn
1 tin tomatoes
2 onions
10 cloves garlic
4 dried shallots
2 spring onions
3 tbsp oil
1 tbsp black pepper
1 cup Simple Brown Sauce (P.93)

Seasoning:
3 tbsp wine
1/2 cup Stock (P.101)
1 tsp salt
2 tbsp sugar
1 tbsp light soy
1/4 tsp pepper
1 tsp sesame oil
2 tbsp cornflour and water mixture

Method:
* Wash and cook the ox-tongue in boiling water for a while. Remove and scrape the membrane off the ox-tongue. Rinse thoroughly under the tap.
* Pour 3 cups of water into a pressure cooker. Add the star anises, peppercorn and 3 slices of ginger and bring to the boil. Put in the ox-tongue and boil for 30 minutes until soft. Turn off the heat and leave the ox-tongue in the pressure cooker for a further 30 minutes. Remove and slice.
* Cut the tinned tomatoes into large pieces, slice the onions, coarsely chop the garlic and shallots, and shred the spring onions.
* Heat the 3 tbsp oil in an earthen pot (or casserole dish), add the remaining 3 slices of ginger and saute the onions, garlic, shallots and tomatoes. Sprinkle in the black pepper and mix well. Stir in the ox-tongue slices. Sizzle the wine, pour in the Stock and the Simple Brown Sauce, mix thoroughly and simmer for 20 minutes over medium heat. Add the rest of the seasoning and stir until the gravy thickens. Serve hot in the casserole dish with the shredded spring onions scattered on top.

材料：
牛脷1條約2磅（1公斤）
薑6片
八角3粒
胡椒粒1茶匙
番茄1罐
洋葱2個
蒜頭10粒
乾葱頭4粒
葱2條
油3湯匙
黑椒粉1湯匙
黃汁1杯（第93頁）

調味：
酒3湯匙
上湯1/2杯（第101頁）
鹽1茶匙
糖2湯匙
生抽1湯匙
胡椒粉1/4茶匙
蔴油1茶匙
生粉水2湯匙

製法：
* 牛脷洗淨後放入沸水中煮片刻，取出刮淨舌苔，再重新沖洗潔淨。
* 壓力煲中注入水數杯，加入一半薑片、八角及胡椒粒煮沸，牛脷放入同煮約1/2小時至軟身，離火焗約1/2小時後取出切片。
* 番茄剪碎，洋葱切片，蒜頭及葱頭切碎，葱切絲。
* 瓦鍋燒熱，加油3湯匙，爆香餘下薑片、洋葱、蒜頭、葱頭、番茄及黑椒，加入牛脷，灒酒炒透，將上湯、黃汁傾下，文火煮20分鐘，加調味料煮成獻，試妥味及灑上葱絲即可原煲上桌。

註：牛脷＝牛舌

Soy Sauce Dip
豉油蘸汁

Ingredients:
2 slices ginger
2 shallots
2 tbsp oil
1/4 tsp salt
1 tbsp wine
1 1/2 cups light soy
1/2 cup dark soy
1 cup sugar
1 chicken cube
1 tsp pepper
1/4 cup sesame oil

Finished Product:
3 cups

Storage Time:
1 month at room temperature
3 months in a refrigerator

Method:
* Peel the ginger and mash it with the shallots.
* Heat a saucepan over medium heat and bring the oil to the boil. Sprinkle in the salt. Saute the ginger and shallots until aromatic and discard. Sprinkle in the wine. Pour in the light soy, dark soy, sugar, and the chicken cube, and return to the boil over low heat. Season to taste. Stir in the pepper and sesame oil. Continue to stir until the liquid reboils. Turn off the heat and leave to cool. Store in a clean bottle.

Usage:
* Soy Sauce Dip is served with plain cooked ingredients, such as blanched beef, ox-tripe, pig's kidney, liver, vegetables and rice sheet rolls, or poured over rice casseroles. Reboil the dip before use.

豉油蘸汁

材料：
薑2片
葱頭2粒
油2湯匙
鹽1/4茶匙
酒1湯匙
生抽1 1/2杯
老抽1/2杯
糖1杯
鷄精1粒
胡椒粉1茶匙
蔴油1/4杯

製成品：
3杯

貯存期：
室溫1月
雪櫃3月

製法：
* 薑刮去皮，與葱頭同拍扁。
* 鍋燒熱，加油煮沸，灑鹽，爆香薑葱頭後棄去。灒酒，傾下生抽、老抽、糖及鷄精，文火煮沸。試妥味後，灑入胡椒粉，再拌入蔴油，煮至重沸時熄去爐火。晾凍，以窄口玻璃瓶盛載，隨時取用。

用途：
* 此汁專用以配白灼肉如：白灼牛肉、白灼牛柏葉及豬腰肝、油菜、豬腸粉等，亦可用以淋在煲仔飯之上。用時將汁煮沸即可。

Healthy Red Rice
保健紅米飯

保健紅米飯

Ingredients:
1 cup red rice
3 cups water
1 cup long grain rice
2 tbsp oil
1 tsp salt
1 tbsp minced garlic
1/4 cup minced onion
4 oz (112g) chicken breast
3 oz (84g) green leek
2 boiled eggwhites
1 cup sweetcorn
2 tbsp minced parsley

Marinade:
1 tsp ginger juice
1 tsp wine
1 tsp cornflour
2 tbsp water
1 tsp light soy

Sauce:
1/3 cup Soy Sauce Dip (P.97)

Method:
* Soak the red rice overnight and drain off excess water. Pour into a saucepan, add 3 cups of water and simmer for 15 minutes over low heat.
* Remove and drain the red rice into a large bowl, retaining 1 1/2 cups of the water for later use. Wash the long grain rice and mix it with the red rice.
* Heat a wok over medium heat and bring the oil to the boil. Sprinkle in the salt and saute the garlic and onion until aromatic. Stir in the mixed rice and fry thoroughly. Transfer to a saucepan and add the 1 1/2 cups of red rice water. Cover with a lid and bring the water to the boil over high heat. Turn to low heat and simmer for another 15 minutes.
* Dice the chicken breast, mix the marinade ingredients thoroughly and soak the chicken in it for 10 minutes. Dice the green leek and boiled eggwhites.
* Remove the lid and pour the diced chicken over the rice. Cover again and cook for a further 8 minutes. Turn off the heat and leave for 8 minutes. Stir in the green leek, sweetcorn and eggwhites. Loosen the rice with a pair of chopsticks and stream in the Soy Sauce Dip. Serve hot, sprinkled with the minced parsley.

材料：
紅米1杯
水3杯
白米1杯
油2湯匙
鹽1茶匙
蒜茸1湯匙
洋葱茸1/4杯
鷄胸肉4安士（112克）
韮菜3安士（84克）
熟蛋白2隻
粟米1杯
芫荽茸2湯匙

醃料：
薑汁1茶匙
酒1茶匙
生粉1茶匙
水2湯匙
生抽1茶匙

淋汁：
豉油蘸汁1/3杯（第97頁）

製法：
* 紅米浸過夜，隔乾水分，用3杯水文火煮15分鐘後隔乾，將米水1 1/2杯留後用，白米洗淨，與隔乾紅米混和。
* 鑊燒熱，將油放入煮沸，加鹽炒香蒜茸及洋葱。隨把米傾下續炒至完全混合，倒入鍋中，加紅米水，以大火煮沸，即改用文火續煮15分鐘。
* 鷄胸切粒，用和勻醃料醃10分鐘。韮菜及蛋白切粒。
* 揭蓋，把鷄粒倒在飯上，再蓋密續煮8分鐘，停火焗8分鐘後，即將韮菜、粟米及蛋白傾在飯上，挑鬆，淋豉油蘸汁及灑芫荽拌勻即可食用。

Stock
上湯

上湯

Ingredients:

1 stewing chicken
8 oz (224g) ham bone
18 cups water
2 slices ginger
2 oz (56g) Chinese celery (sectioned)
4 spring onions (sectioned)
1 tsp salt

Finished Product:

8 cups

Storage Time:

1 month in a refrigerator
3 months in a freezer

Method:

* Peel the skin off the chicken and blanch together with the bone. Clean and drain for later use.

* Pour the water into a saucepan and bring to the boil. Add the ginger, Chinese celery, spring onions, chicken and bone and cook over high heat until it reboils. Reduce to low heat and simmer for 3 hours. Filter the Stock and season with salt. Adjust the flavour to taste. Leave to cool, then store in a plastic box for future use.

Usage:

* The Stock has many uses. It is used as a base for making gravy for meat dishes and is excellent for blanching green vegetables in order to retain the vitamins and nutrients. The Stock on its own is a nutritious healthy soup.

材料：

老鷄1隻
火腿骨1/2磅（224克）
水18杯
薑2片
中芹2安士（切段）
葱4條（切段）
鹽1茶匙

製成品：

8杯

貯存期：

雪櫃1月
冰箱3月

製法：

* 老鷄去皮後與火腿骨同置沸水中飛水，盛起洗淨隔乾候用。

* 深煲中注入水煮沸，加薑片、中芹、葱、老鷄及火腿骨猛火煮至重沸後，改用文火續煮3小時，隔去渣，加鹽調至合味，晾凍後入盒。

用途：

* 上湯用途甚廣，可用以製作任何肉類之獻汁，亦可用以速燙青菜以保存維他命及營養素，更可作補身之湯水。

註：飛水＝迅速浸於沸水中令鷄皮收縮及去除腥味。

Sweetcorn Sauce
粟米汁

粟米汁

Ingredients:

2 slices ginger
2 shallots
3 tbsp oil
2 tins sweetcorn

Seasoning:

1 tsp wine
3 cups Stock (P.101)
1/4 tsp salt
1/2 tsp pepper
3 tbsp cornflour and water mix
1 tsp sesame oil

Finished Product:

6 cups

Storage Time:

3 days in a refrigerator
1 month in a freezer

Method:

* Peel, clean and mash the ginger and shallots.
* Heat a wok and bring the oil to the boil. Saute the ginger and shallots until aromatic, then discard. Sizzle the wine, pour in the Stock and bring to the boil again. Add the sweetcorn and the seasoning. Thicken the sauce with the cornflour and water mixture and blend in the sesame oil. Leave to cool and store in a jar. Keep in a freezer.

Usage:

* Sweetcorn Sauce is best served with deep fried dishes including fish, chicken and pork chop. It can also be blended with eggwhite and poured onto steamed rice.

材料：

薑2片
葱頭2粒
油3湯匙
粟米2罐

調味：

酒1茶匙
上湯3杯（第101頁）
鹽1/4茶匙
胡椒粉1/2茶匙
生粉水3湯匙
蔴油1茶匙

製成品：

6杯

貯存期：

雪櫃3天
冰箱1月

製法：

* 薑與去衣葱頭洗淨，一同拍扁候用。
* 燒紅鑊，加油煮沸，放入葱、薑爆香，棄去。灒酒，加上湯煮沸，隨將粟米倒入煮片刻，加調味料試妥味，以生粉水慢慢流入和成獻汁，加蔴油拌勻，晾凍後以闊口瓶盛載，轉置冰箱內貯存。

用途：

* 粟米汁多用於油炸食品如炸魚塊、雞扒、豬扒等，亦可用以淋於熱飯上。和獻後加入蛋白拌勻即可。

註：豬扒＝豬排　粟米＝玉米

Steamed Rice with Crab Meat in Sweetcorn Sauce 粟米蟹肉燴飯

粟米蟹肉燴飯

Ingredients:
2 eggwhites
3 cups hot steamed rice
2 tbsp oil
1 cup Sweetcorn Sauce (P.103)
4 oz (112g) crab meat
1 tbsp diced spring onion
Seasoning:
1 tsp wine
1/3 cup Stock (P.101)
1/2 tsp sugar
1/4 tsp pepper
Gravy:
1 tsp cornflour
1 tbsp water
1 tsp sesame oil
Method:
* Whisk the eggwhites. Dish the hot steamed rice on to a platter.
* Heat a wok and bring the oil to the boil. Sizzle the wine, pour in the Stock and bring to the boil again. Stir in the Sweetcorn Sauce and seasoning.
* Blend the cornflour and water together, slowly stream the mixture into the wok and thicken to a gravy. Stir in the eggwhites and crab meat. Sprinkle the sesame oil and mask the sauce over the rice. Scatter the spring onion on top and serve immediately.

材料：
蛋白2隻
熱飯3杯
油2湯匙
粟米汁1杯（第103頁）
蟹肉4安士（112克）
葱粒1湯匙
調味：
酒1茶匙
上湯1/3杯（第101頁）
糖1/2茶匙
胡椒粉1/4茶匙
獻料：
生粉1茶匙
水1湯匙
蔴油1茶匙（後下）
製法：
* 蛋白打勻，熱飯盛在熱碟上。
* 燒紅鑊，加油煮沸，灒酒，加上湯煮滾，傾入粟米汁及調味料，試妥味。
* 生粉加水混合後，慢慢流入粟米汁中煮至濃度適中，即放入蛋白，加蟹肉、蔴油拌勻，淋在熱飯上，灑葱粒上桌。

Sweet and Sour Sauce
糖醋汁

Ingredients:
2 slices ginger
2 tbsp oil
1 1/2 cups white vinegar
2 cups cane sugar (or brown sugar)
1 cup chilli tomato sauce
2 tsp chicken powder
1/4 tsp salt
2 tbsp red food colouring solution (optional)

Finished Product:
4 cups

Storage Time:
3 months at room temperature
6 months in a refrigerator

Method:
* Mash the ginger. Bring the oil to the boil in a saucepan over high heat. Saute the ginger until pungent and discard.
* Blend all the ingredients together and pour the mixture into the saucepan. Return to the boil.
* Leave to cool and store in a jar.
* Before use, reheat the Sweet and Sour Sauce. For every 1/2 cup of sauce, blend 1 tsp cornflour with 1 tbsp water to a smooth cream and thicken the sauce to a gravy.

Usage:
* Sweet and Sour Sauce is best used as a dipping sauce for deep fried meat and fish fillet, or as a gravy for steamed fish.

糖醋汁

材料：
薑2片
油2湯匙
白醋1 1/2杯
原蔗糖2杯
辣茄汁1杯
雞粉2茶匙
鹽1/4茶匙
紅粉水2湯匙（隨意）

製成品：
4杯

貯存期：
室溫3月
雪櫃6月

製法：
* 薑拍扁，油煮沸，將薑放入炸香棄去。
* 隨將全部材料混和傾入煮沸。
* 晾凍後流入瓶中貯存，用時每1/2杯糖醋汁加生粉1茶匙與水1湯匙和勻作獻汁即可。

用途：
* 此汁除可配魚塊外，更可與任何炸肉配合，亦可作蒸活魚之獻汁。

Fish Fillet in Sweet and Sour Sauce
糖醋魚塊

糖醋魚塊

Ingredients:
10 oz (280g) fish fillet
1 egg
1 cup cornflour
1/2 wok oil
1 shallot
1 garlic

Marinade:
1 tsp light soy
1/2 tsp sugar
1/2 tsp pepper
1/2 eggwhite
1/2 tsp sesame oil

Seasoning
1 tsp wine
1/2 cup Sweet and Sour Sauce (P.107)
1/2 tsp sugar
1 tsp cornflour
1 tbsp water

Method:
* Clean, dry and slice the fish into thin pieces. Mix the marinade ingredients thoroughly and immerse the fish in it for 15 minutes. Turn over and marinate the other side for a further 15 minutes.
* Beat the egg in a separate bowl and sift the cornflour onto a dish. Remove the fish slices from the marinade and coat each evenly with the beaten egg. Then dredge with the cornflour and press tightly.
* Bring the oil to the boil in a wok over medium heat and deep fry the fish slices until golden brown. Drain and arrange on a platter.
* Slice the shallot and garlic. Clean and reheat the wok, put in 2 tbsp of the remaining oil and bring it to the boil. Saute the shallot and garlic until fragrant. Sizzle the wine, pour in the Sweet and Sour Sauce and bring to the boil. Reduce to low heat, add the sugar and simmer until it dissolves. Season to taste. Blend the cornflour and water to a smooth cream in a separate bowl, trickle the mixture into the wok to thicken the Sweet and Sour Sauce. Scoop it over the deep fried fish slices and serve.

材料：
魚柳10安士（280克）
蛋1隻
生粉1杯
油1/2鑊
葱頭1粒
蒜頭1粒

醃料：
生抽1茶匙
糖1/2茶匙
胡椒粉1/2茶匙
蛋白1/2隻
蔴油1/2茶匙

調味：
酒1茶匙
糖醋汁1/2杯（第107頁）
糖1/2茶匙
生粉1茶匙
水1湯匙

製法：
* 魚柳略洗後抹乾，切成薄片，放入已和勻之醃料中醃15分鐘，反轉再醃15分鐘。
* 蛋打散，將魚放入蘸滿蛋液，再蘸生粉，以手略壓使生粉貼緊。
* 油燒沸，將魚塊放入炸至金黃色，盛起，隔去餘油，排放在碟上。
* 葱頭、蒜頭切片，鑊燒熱，加餘油2湯匙煮沸，放入葱、蒜片爆香。灒酒，傾下糖醋汁煮沸，轉慢火加入其餘調味料試妥味，淋在魚塊上即成。

Szchuen Piquant Sauce

魚香汁

魚香汁

Ingredients:
1/8 oz (3.5g) black fungus
2 oz (56g) water chestnuts
3 slices ginger
1/2 oz (14g) garlic
4 red chillies
1 spring onion
2 tbsp oil
2 cups Stock (P.101)
1/2 cup hot broad bean paste
1/4 cup tomato ketchup
3 tbsp light soy
3 tbsp sugar
2 tbsp vinegar
1 tbsp cornflour
2 tbsp water
1/4 tsp dark soy
2 tbsp sesame oil

Finished Product:
3 cups

Storage Time:
2 days at room temperature
2 weeks in a refrigerator

Method:
* Soak, trim and blanch the black fungus. Refresh and dice finely.
* Peel, wash and mince the waterchestnuts. Mince the ginger and garlic. Deseed the chillies, wash the spring onion and dice both ingredients.
* Heat a stainless-steel saucepan or earthen pot over medium heat. Bring the oil to the boil and saute the minced ginger and garlic until pungent. Stir in the black fungus, water chestnuts and chillies and fry well. Pour in the Stock and seasoning and bring to the boil. Mix the cornflour, water, dark soy and sesame oil in a separate bowl, trickle the mixture into the sauce and thicken to a gravy. Leave to cool and store in a jar.

Usage:
* This is an all-purpose sauce which can be used with meat, seafood and vegetables such as broccoli and cauliflower.

材料：
木耳1/8安士（3.5克）
馬蹄2安士（56克）
薑3片
蒜頭1/2安士（14克）
紅椒4隻
葱1棵
油2湯匙
上湯2杯（第101頁）
豆瓣醬1/2杯
茄汁1/4杯
生抽3湯匙
糖3湯匙
醋2湯匙
生粉1湯匙
水2湯匙
老抽1/4茶匙
蔴油2湯匙

製成品：
3杯

貯存期：
室溫2天
雪櫃2周

製法
* 木耳浸透去硬蒂，飛水沖凍切細粒。（飛水即以沸水浸片刻撈起。）
* 馬蹄去皮洗淨切細，薑片、蒜頭皆剁茸。紅椒去籽，葱洗淨，一同切粒候用。
* 煲中加油煮沸，爆香薑、蒜茸後，放入木耳、馬蹄及紅椒炒片刻。傾入上湯及其他調味料。待煮沸後，以生粉加水、老抽及蔴油拌勻，滴入混合料中和成濃汁。晾凍盛在瓶內，隨時取用。

用途：
* 此汁用途甚廣，除與肉類、海鮮同煮外，更可配以蔬菜如西蘭花、椰菜花等。

註：馬蹄=荸薺　木耳=黑木耳　西蘭花=青花菜　椰菜花=白花菜

Prawns in Piquant Sauce

魚香鳳尾蝦

魚香鳳尾蝦

Ingredients:
12 king prawns
1 slice ginger
2 shallots
2 cloves garlic
1/2 wok oil
2 parsley sprigs
cooked broccoli to garnish

Seasoning:
1/4 tsp salt
1 tsp wine
1/2 cup Piquant Sauce (P.111)
1/4 cup Stock (P.101)
1/2 tsp cornflour + 1/2 tsp water

Method:
* Shell and devein the prawns, retaining the shell towards the end of the tails.
* Mince the ginger, shallots and garlic.
* Parboil the prawns in hot oil until they curl up. Drain thoroughly.
* Retain 1 tbsp oil in the wok and reboil. Scatter salt and saute the ginger, shallots and garlic until aromatic. Add the prawns and sizzle wine. Pour in the Piquant Sauce, Stock & cornflour mixture, and stir fry for a while. Adjust the flavour to taste and dish. Garnish with parsley and broccoli.

Usage:
* This is an appetizing and appealing dish in family cooking. To avoid excess fat, the parboiling procedure can be omitted and the prawns can be stir-fried with the other ingredients.

材料：
大蝦12隻
薑1片
葱頭2粒
蒜頭2粒
油1/2鍋
芫荽2棵（裝飾）
熟西蘭花（裝飾）

調味：
鹽1/4茶匙
酒1茶匙
魚香汁1/2杯（第111頁）
上湯1/4杯（第101頁）
生粉水1茶匙

製法：
* 蝦從頭去殼挑腸，將背部略剔開，留下蝦尾殼完整。
* 薑、葱、蒜剁茸。
* 油煮熱，將蝦放入泡浸至捲起，盛起隔去油。
* 鍋中油傾回油桶內，只餘1湯匙油煮沸，灑鹽爆香薑葱蒜茸，至香味四溢時，把蝦回鑊，濳酒，傾下魚香汁、上湯及生粉水拌炒片刻，試妥味後灑芫荽，上碟，以西蘭花伴碟。

用途：
* 此為色香味俱佳之家常小菜。如不欲將蝦泡油，則可直接與各細粒同炒至捲起即可。

註：馬蹄＝荸薺　西蘭花＝青花菜

Thousand Island Sauce
千島汁

千島汁

Ingredients:

1 oz (28g) pickled ginger
4 eggs
2 1/4 cups salad cream
1 1/4 cups tomato ketchup
1/2 tsp black pepper
1/2 tsp white pepper
3 tsp sugar

Finished Product:

4 cups

Storage Time:

1 week in a refrigerator

Method:

* Finely dice the pickled ginger and place in a mixing bowl.
* Put the eggs in a saucepan half-filled with water. Cover and bring it to the boil over low heat. Remove the lid and continue to boil the eggs for another 5 minutes. Take out the eggs and rinse under a tap until completely cold. Shell and dice the boiled eggs and put them in the mixing bowl.
* Blend in the salad cream and tomato ketchup, then sprinkle with the black pepper, white pepper and sugar. Mix thoroughly, adjust the flavour to taste and store in a jar.

Usage:

* This sauce can be mixed with salads or served as a dip for deep fried fish and other deep fried seafood.

材料：

酸子薑1安士（28克）
鷄蛋4隻
沙律醬2 1/4杯
茄汁1 1/4杯
黑椒粉1/2茶匙
胡椒粉1/2茶匙
糖3茶匙

製成品：

4杯

貯存期：

雪櫃1周

製法：

* 酸子薑剁細粒，放在大盆中候用。
* 鷄蛋置半鍋水中以文火煮至水沸，開蓋續煮5分鐘，將蛋取出，放水喉下沖凍，去殼後切細粒放在盆中。
* 沙律醬與茄汁同傾入盆中，灑黑椒粉、胡椒粉及糖一同拌勻，試妥味即可入瓶隨時取用。

用途：

* 此汁除用於拌製沙律之外，可配炸魚及炸海鮮等。

註：子薑=嫩薑　沙律醬=沙拉醬

Tri-Colour Crab Rolls
三色蟹柳卷

三色蟹柳卷

Ingredients:

Pastry-

12 sheets rice pastry
1/2 cup Coca Cola
1/2 cup water
1/4 tsp bicarbonate soda

Filling-

1 egg
8 oz (224g) cucumber
6 crab sticks

Seasoning:

1/2 tsp salt
1/2 tsp sugar
1/2 tsp chicken powder
1/4 tsp pepper
1/2 tsp sesame oil
1/2 beaten egg

To Complete:

1 egg yolk for sealing
1/2 wok oil

Served With:

1/2 cup Thousand Island Sauce (P.115)
12 Chinese lettuce leaves
12 mint leaves

Method:

Filling-

* Beat one egg and fry in a pan until set. Leave to cool and then shred.

* Finely shred the cucumber and tear the crab sticks into shreds. Put the shredded egg, cucumber, crab sticks and all the seasoning into mixing bowl and blend the ingredients thoroughly.

Pastry-

* Mix the Coca Cola, water and bicarbonate soda thoroughly and brush the mixture on to each sheet of rice pastry. Towel dry and fold each sheet in half. Place 2 tbsp filling on one side of the pastry. Roll it up, fold in both ends and seal it with the beaten egg yolk.

To complete-

* Heat a wok over high heat and bring the oil to the boil. Slide in the rolls and deep fry until golden brown. Drain and arrange them on a plate. Serve with the Chinese lettuce, mint and Thousand Island Sauce.

材料：

皮一
越南春卷皮12張
可樂汽水1/2杯
水1/2杯
梳打粉1/4茶匙

餡一
鷄蛋1隻
青瓜8安士（224克）
蟹柳6條

調味：

鹽1/2茶匙
糖1/2茶匙
鷄粉1/2茶匙
胡椒粉1/4茶匙
蔴油1/2茶匙
鷄蛋1/2隻

完成：

蛋黃1隻（封口）
油1/2鍋

伴食：

千島汁1/2杯（第115頁）
唐生菜12片
香花菜12塊

製法：

* 餡一鷄蛋去殼打爛，放煎鑊內煎成蛋皮，晾凍後切絲。

* 青瓜切絲，蟹柳撕細。鷄蛋、青瓜及蟹柳與調味料拌勻。

* 皮一可樂、水及梳打粉拌勻，掃在春卷皮上再用毛巾抹乾，將每張皮對摺成半月形，包入餡料捲起，用蛋黃封口。

* 完成一燒熱油，放入春卷炸至金黃色即可上碟。伴以唐生菜、香花菜及千島汁。

註：青瓜=黃瓜　唐生菜=中國萵苣菜

Wine and Oyster Sauce
紹酒蠔油汁

紹酒蠔油汁

Ingredients:
1 slice ginger
1 shallot
1 clove garlic
1 tbsp oil
1/2 tsp salt
1 cup yellow wine
1/2 cup water
1/4 cup oyster sauce
3 tbsp light soy
3 tbsp sugar
1 chicken cube
1/2 tsp pepper

Finished Product:
2 cups

Storage Time:
2 weeks in a refrigerator
3 months in a freezer

Method:
* Peel and mince the ginger, shallot and garlic.
* Heat a saucepan, pour in the oil and salt and saute the minced ingredients until aromatic. Sprinkle in the yellow wine, then blend in the water.
* Mix the remaining seasoning in a bowl and stream the mixture into the saucepan. Stir evenly and adjust the flavour to taste. Remove and leave to cool.

Usage:
* This sauce can be served with stewed chicken and pigeon, and can be used as a dip for Won Ton with Ginger and Spring Onions.

材料：
薑1片
葱、蒜頭各1粒
油1湯匙
鹽1/2茶匙
花雕1杯
水1/2杯
蠔油1/4杯
生抽3湯匙
糖3湯匙
鷄精1粒
胡椒粉1/2茶匙

製成品：
2杯

貯存期：
雪櫃2周
冰箱3月

製法：
* 薑、葱、蒜去皮剁成茸。
* 鍋燒熱，加油灑鹽煮沸，爆香薑、葱、蒜。濽下紹酒將水傾入。
* 調味料放碗中混和，流入鍋中拌勻，試至合味，即可盛起待用。

用途：
* 此汁除可用於焗鷄及乳鴿外，亦可與薑葱雲吞配食。

註：花雕＝紹酒

淮杞花雕鷄

Ingredients:
1 chicken, about 3 lb (1 1/2kg)
2 oz (56g) common yam rhizome (Wai Shan)
2 slices ginger
3 shallots
1 tbsp oil
1 oz (28g) medlar
2 tbsp chopped parsley

Marinade:
1 tbsp ginger juice
1/4 cup yellow wine
2 tbsp light soy
1 tbsp sugar
1 tbsp cornflour

Seasoning:
1 cup Wine and Oyster Sauce (P.119)
1/2 cup Stock (P.101)
1 tsp dark soy

Method:
* Rinse and chop the chicken into serving pieces. Immerse in the marinade for 30 minutes, then deep fry in the oil over low heat and drain, retaining 1 tbsp oil for later use.
* Boil the common yam rhizome in 1/2 cup water until it turns transparent. Shred the ginger and slice the shallots.
* Bring the 1 tbsp oil to the boil in a casserole dish and saute the ginger and shallots until aromatic. Pour in the chicken and common yam rhizome and stir fry for 2 minutes. Add the Wine and Oyster Sauce and stew, covered, for 10 minutes. Remove the lid, turn over the chicken pieces and common yam rhizome, stir in the medlar and simmer for a further 2 minutes. Season to taste and sprinkle with parsley then serve.

Tips:
* For best results, choose a spring chicken of under 4 lb (2 kg).
* A fat, young pigeon can also be used instead of a chicken.
* Ginger juice and wine are important ingredients for removing the raw smell of the poultry. Ginger powder and brandy can be used as a substitute.
* Medlar and common yam rhizome can be replaced by onion.

材料：
鷄1隻3磅（1 1/2公斤）
淮山2安士（56克）
薑2片
葱頭3粒
油1湯匙
杞子1安士（28克）
芫荽2湯匙

醃料：
薑汁1湯匙
紹酒1/4杯
生抽2湯匙
糖1湯匙
生粉1湯匙

調味：
紹酒蠔油汁1杯（第119頁）
上湯1/2杯（第101頁）
老抽1茶匙

製法：
* 鷄洗淨斬件，以和勻醃料醃1/2小時，泡油盛起隔乾。
* 淮山用水1/2杯煮至透明，薑切絲，葱頭切片。
* 瓦鍋燒熱，加油煮沸，將薑絲、葱片放入爆香。隨把鷄件傾下拌勻，即加淮山同炒片刻。傾入紹酒蠔油汁，蓋密鍋蓋以文火燜10分鐘，揭蓋將鷄件淮山翻動後，灑下杞子再燜2分鐘。試妥味灑芫荽原鍋上桌。

烹飪秘訣：
* 此菜宜選用4磅（2公斤）以下黃油嫩鷄。
* 肥嫩乳鴿可作鷄之代用品。
* 薑汁及酒有去禽鳥腥味之作用，如無薑汁紹酒可用薑粉及拔蘭地代替。
* 若無淮山杞子，可以洋葱代之。

Chicken in Wine and Oyster Sauce

淮杞花鵰雞

STORAGE OF DIPS AND SAUCES

醬汁貯存法

1. **Polythene Cup Storage** - Wash some plastic cups of different sizes (1/2 cup, 1 cup and 2 cups) and sterilise them thoroughly twice with boiling water. Stream in the cooled sauce, and clearly mark its name and production date on the outside of the cup.
2. **Ice-tray Storage** - Wash and boil the ice-tray in a wok of boiling water. Dry the tray and pour in the sauce. Set aside to cool, then place in a freezer where the sauce will freeze into cubes. Wrap the ice-tray in cling film and store it in a plastic bag. To use the sauce, remove the bag and cling film, pour cold water onto the bottom of the ice-tray and tap out the frozen cubes of sauce.
3. **Ice Ball Bottle Storage** - This is a special kind of plastic bottle used for making ball-shaped "ice cubes". Stream in the cooled sauce then seal tightly and store in a freezer. To use, place the ice ball bottle under a cold running tap to loosen the balls of sauce. Remove them as needed. To prevent the bottle from cracking, place it in a zipper freezer bag.
4. **Plastic Bag Storage** - To use this method, deep freeze the sauce in an ice-tray overnight. Remove and pour water onto the bottom of the ice-tray and tap out the cubes of sauce. Divide them into 4 fl oz (1/2 cup) portions and store each portion in a separate transparent plastic bag or a zipper freezer bag.
5. **Freezer Box Storage** - High quality plastic boxes with air-tight lids must be used for storing sauces. Different size boxes can be used according to the size of your family. For example, 1/4 to 1/2 cup of sauce is sufficient for two people, while six will need 1 to 1 1/2 cups of sauce for one meal.
6. **Glass Bottle or Jar Storage** - Glass bottles should be used for keeping sauces at room temperature or in a refrigerator. They are especially suitable for storing sauces containing vinegar such as Sweet and Sour Sauce.
7. **Microwave-box Storage** - Microwave-boxes can be put straight into a microwave oven direct from a freezer. They are very convenient for working people who have little spare time for cooking. Since the microwave-boxes do not have air-tight lids, they must be wrapped in zipper freezer bags for storage.

Remove the bag before putting the box in a microwave oven.

8. **Used-Carton Storage** - The environmentally conscious can recycle clean used-cartons such as ice-cream boxes or margarine containers for freezer storage. These cartons are not as sturdy as plastic boxes and do not have air-tight lids, so they must be wrapped in zipper freezer bags before storing in a freezer. Sauces can only be stored for a short time using this method.

Whatever container you use for storing food, the storage process must be quick. As soon as the dip or sauce is cooked, it must be cooled and stored in the freezer immediately. Strong-smelling sauces should be double-wrapped in freezer bags to prevent their lively flavours from spoiling other foods.

By following these instructions carefully, you can have tasty sauces with your meals without spending a great deal of time in the kitchen.

1. **膠杯貯存**——預先將1/2杯、1杯及2杯各種不同大小之杯子洗淨，再以沸水將杯內沖洗2次，保證細菌滅絕，然後再把已晾凍之醬汁傾入，標上汁名，並註明製作日期。

2. **冰格貯存**——洗淨冰格，放於沸水鍋內煮1分鐘以消滅細菌，隔乾水分後，將醬汁注入，晾凍，轉放冰箱冷凍成硬塊，以保鮮紙包裹後再放膠袋中貯存。用時取出，以水沖冰格底部，再略敲數下令硬塊鬆出，即可使用。

3. **冰袋貯存**——此為一種壓有圓形空間之膠袋，專為製冰粒而造。把汁晾凍，注入袋封密，放冰箱內冷凍至硬後取出，沖水或略敲即可，用多少取多少，極為方便。為免破裂，可再包一層密實袋。

4. **膠袋貯存**——採用膠袋貯存，必須預早將醬或汁注入冰格內，轉放冰箱中過夜後取出，用水在冰格底略沖，鬆出放在膠袋中。分量可參照自己普通用量分別存放。最佳辦法是將汁分作每4安士（1/2杯）一包存放，以便容易計算及取用。

5. **膠盒貯存**——必須選用無臭味之優質產品，否則貯存後醬汁變味，而且必須選用不同容量之膠盒，以適應不同之家庭。例如二人世界只需選用1/4至1/2杯之汁料，已足夠應付每餐所需；若是一家六口，則要採用較大之膠盒如1杯、1 1/2杯及2杯等等。

6. **玻璃瓶貯存**——玻璃瓶適宜用於可在室溫或雪櫃貯存之醬汁，尤其是帶酸味之汁液。例如甜酸醋、微辣糖醋等，都應以玻璃瓶盛載。

7. **微波盒貯存**——由於此種盒子可直接自冰箱取出，立刻放於微波爐解凍至煮沸，對分秒必爭之職業人士方便非常。但因微波盒蓋子不能密封，所以在注入醬汁後，必須再以密實袋包裹妥當。入爐前把膠袋除出即可。

8. **雜物盒貯存**——對大多數環保人士來說，最佳辦法是保留一些牛油或雪糕盒、芝士盒子等洗淨後廢物利用，用後以沸水沖洗抹乾，將醬汁貯存。但因此種盒蓋並不能蓋緊，所以必須再加一個密實袋包裹妥當作短期貯存。

無論採用任何膠袋或膠盒，貯存必須迅速。任何食物晾凍後必須馬上入瓶或盒，再轉放冰箱。氣味濃烈的如蒜頭、洋葱等必須雙層包裹，以免辛香味被其他材料吸收而受影響。

若能小心處理，醬汁可以助你將每日三餐化繁為簡，使你盡享烹調之樂！

學員廚房活動

STUDENTS KITCHEN ACTIVITIES

1

2

3

4

5

6

7

8

9

10

11

1. Everyone takes part in bread-making.
2. Look, our products aren't half bad.
3. Baking a cake is not so difficult after all.
4. Even tourists take time out to learn Chinese cooking while they're in Hong Kong.
5. See how absorbed these Japanese students are.
6. I didn't realise that a Chinese wok is so heavy.
7. We learn to use the new products before they hit the market.
8. The Filipino maids are keen to learn Chinese cooking.
9. Our Israeli student learns to pick up a wok and turner.
10. Wow! We've finally learned how to toss a wok.
11. Before cooking, we have to learn about the ingredients.
12. Students and teacher making Green Leek Won Ton together.

12

1. 大家動手做麪包。
2. 看看我們的產品也不錯吧！
3. 烘蛋糕原來並不是那麼困難的。
4. 來港觀光也不放過學習中國菜式之機會。
5. 且看日本同學的投入情況。
6. 中國鑊原來是那麼重的！
7. 產品推出市場前先來學習產品之用途。
8. 菲傭對中菜的興趣也不弱呢！
9. 以色列同學放下鎗桿也來學習拿鑊鏟了。
10. 啊！我們結果學懂了拋鑊。
11. 未開始製作前，先了解一下材料之組合。
12. 師徒齊來製作韮菜雲吞。

博益

醬汁食譜

作　者　歐陽紉澌
編　輯　博益編輯委員會
責任編輯　黃麗儀
美術設計　李春培
攝　影　嘉饌出版有限公司
出版 / 發行　博益出版集團有限公司
香港禮頓道一號
2836-6088
印　刷　海洋印務有限公司
出版日期　二○○○年三月（第二版）
出版書號　7R 31308
ISBN　962-17-1142-8

A SCMP Publication
南華早報出版物
Printed in Hong Kong